Book-keeping and Accounts

For Entrepreneurs

Books that make you better

Books that make you better. That make you *be* better,
do better, *feel* better. Whether you want to upgrade your
personal skills or change your job, whether you want to improve
your managerial style, become a more powerful communicator,
or be stimulated and inspired as you work.

Prentice Hall Business is leading the field with a new breed of
skills, careers and development books. Books that are a cut
above the mainstream – in topic, content and delivery – with an
edge and verve that will make you better, with less effort.

Books that are as sharp and smart as you are.

Prentice Hall Business.
We work harder – so you don't have to.

For more details on products, and to contact us, visit
www.pearsoned.co.uk

Book-keeping and Accounts

For Entrepreneurs

Martin Quinn

PEARSON
Prentice Hall
BUSINESS

Harlow, England • London • New York • Boston • San Francisco • Toronto • Sydney • Singapore • Hong Kong
Tokyo • Seoul • Taipei • New Delhi • Cape Town • Madrid • Mexico City • Amsterdam • Munich • Paris • Milan

PEARSON EDUCATION LIMITED

Edinburgh Gate
Harlow CM20 2JE
Tel: +44 (0)1279 623623
Fax: +44 (0)1279 431059
Website: www.pearsoned.co.uk

First published in Great Britain in 2010

ISBN: 978-0-273-72395-0

British Library Cataloguing-in-Publication Data
A catalogue record for this book is available from the British Library

Library of Congress Cataloging-in-Publication Data
A catalog record for this book is available from the Library of Congress

10 9 8 7 6 5 4 3 2 1
13 12 11 10 09

Screenshots on pages 65, 66, 67, 68, 69, 87, 89, 110, 111 and 112 © Intuit. All rights reserved.
Series text design by Design Delux
Typeset in 9/13pt Swis721 Lt BT by 30
Printed and bound in Great Britain by Ashford Colour Press Ltd., Gosport

The Publisher's policy is to use paper manufactured from sustainable forests.

Contents

This book is dedicated to my family – my wife Regina, and our children, Josephina and Eric.

...for Entrepreneurs

Being an entrepreneur can be the path to controlling your own life and to financial success. With the *For Entrepreneurs* series, it doesn't have to be a lonely journey any more. Our expert authors guide you through all phases of starting and running a business, with practical advice every step of the way. Whether you are just getting started or want to grow your business, whether you want to become a skilled marketer or salesperson or just want to get your business finances under control, there is a *For Entrepreneurs* book ready to be your experienced friendly and supportive business coach. Our titles include:

→ *How to Start Your Own Business for Entrepreneurs*
→ *How to Grow Your Business for Entrepreneurs*
→ *Selling for Entrepreneurs*
→ *Marketing for Entrepreneurs*
→ *Book-keeping and Accounts for Entrepreneurs*

You'll find more information and more support on our website: **www.forentrepreneursbooks.com**.

Jurgen Wolff, General Editor

About the author

Martin Quinn is a Chartered Management Accountant and a lecturer in accounting at Dublin City University, Dublin, Ireland. He has spent 15 years working in small and large companies as a management accountant, preparing the reports and information managers need to make decisions. He has also worked with many first-time entrepreneurs, helping them to get their business started and, once going, to manage it by keeping a good eye on 'the numbers'. More importantly, Martin encourages entrepreneurs from day one not to be reliant on their accountant, by having a good grasp of accounting issues in their own business.

Acknowledgements

Thanks to everyone who has helped me hone my knowledge of accounting over the years. Many thanks also to my colleagues at Dublin City University for helping me to learn how to impart this knowledge and encourage others to learn.

Thanks also to Sam and Matthew at Pearson for helping me get this book into print. Many thanks also to Jurgen Wolff, the series editor, for his useful comments and editing.

Introduction

Accounting isn't the most glamorous part of setting up or running a business. Most entrepreneurs would rather spend their time developing their product line or growing their client base. But accounting is important. Without it, your business will never reach its full potential. A lack of adequate accounting could even create legal problems that could easily have been avoided.

As an entrepreneur you like to conceive an idea, set up a business, and watch it grow. Most likely, maximising profits is one of your goals. Unfortunately, many businesses lose money. How can this be avoided? One key element is tracking the costs of your business. This, of course, requires that often dreaded task – accounting.

Accounting is usually viewed as a boring, complex and technical subject understood only by those who have completed accounting or business degrees. However, accounting, no matter how complex it becomes, has a very simple set of principles as its background. Knowledge of the fundamentals will not make you a fully-fledged accountant, but you will begin to understand that the subject is, after all, quite simple. As an entrepreneur, you don't need to know all the rules and terminology. Also, practising what you know improves your skills. By immediately applying what you learn from this book to your business, you will learn what you need to know at the same time as you improve your bottom line.

The purpose of accounting is twofold:

→ First, a basic business accounting system records the receipts and expenditures of the day-to-day activities of a business. This data is vital for the completion of your annual tax returns and other legal documents. It will also be required by lenders when you apply for a small business loan.

→ Second, it provides you – the entrepreneur – with a valuable tool for assessing and analysing the performance of your business. With just a little practice you will begin to notice trends that highlight your business's strengths and weaknesses. This information will help you make informed decisions about how to improve your bottom line.

Before you start your business venture

Part One

Accounting fundamentals

Chapter One

In this chapter, I explain the basic 'must know' concepts of accounting for any business owner or entrepreneur who wants to (1) do their own accounts; or (2) converse with accountants in a meaningful way. What you read here will be used again and again throughout the rest of the book. Take your time with this chapter and refer back to it if you need to. Don't worry, there are no numbers to master. You need to get a good grasp of the fundamentals first.

The nature, purpose and role of accounting

If you look at definitions of accounting you will get something like: 'the systematic recording, reporting and analysis of the financial transactions of a business'. The word 'record' or 'collect' is usually there – this is the book-keeping part of accounting where business data is captured and recorded. You will also see words like 'collate' or 'report' which refer to the bringing together of data in a format which is usable, like the income statement and balance sheet. Lastly, you will also come across words like 'monetary' or 'financial', suggesting that accounting is concerned only with transactions which have a money value attached to them.

The final part of the definition indicates that someone will analyse accounting information. In other words, accounting produces information which will be communicated. Accounting is often described as the 'language of business'. Like a spoken language, the better your understanding, the better your ability to communicate with those who use the language. Accounting information must be communicated to those who make the decisions in the business, perhaps the owner or board of directors. The information includes things like:

→ whether the business is making a profit or a loss;

→ what a business is worth;

→ how much cash is in a business;

→ how much a business is owed and how much it owes;

→ how the business is performing.

To summarise, the purpose of accounting is the provision of information to decision-makers. Later, I will explain the types of users of accounting information in more detail.

Branches of accounting

Accountants perform many functions. If you have used the services of an accountant you may know that they offer book-keeping, accounts preparation, taxation and audit services. At this stage you should know the two main branches of accounting, namely financial accounting and management accounting.

Financial accounting

This branch deals mainly with book-keeping and accounts preparation (both are explained in more detail in later chapters). Financial accounting is concerned primarily with the production of accounting information for people external to the business. Quite a lot of the work in financial accounting is driven by legislation like tax or company law. The information produced is highly aggregated and summarised. Finally, the information is normally based on historic data (for example, total sales revenue last year) and must be accurate

Management accounting

As the term suggests, management accounting is more concerned with the information needs of managers within the business. Managers need information on a much more regular basis than anyone else. They also need more detailed information; for example, the revenue generated by each product or customer. Decisions may also be based on information which is nothing more than a best guess or gut-feeling: for example, sales of a new product. Thus, compared to financial accounting, management accounting information tends to be less structured, more detailed and often based on estimates. This is not to say that management accountants do not do financial accounting work – they do – but their main purpose is to provide whatever information is necessary to help managers make day-to-day decisions.

Here's an example of the difference between the two branches. You will find financial accountants in a typical accounting practice. They will perform book-keeping tasks for you on a regular basis (monthly, perhaps) and prepare accounts and tax returns for you at the end of each year. Management accountants work within a business. Each day they keep an eye on key figures in the business. They may work with other accounting staff, who do the book-keeping work on a daily basis. With someone else working on the detail, management accountants can provide whatever ad hoc information managers require. They will prepare plans and budgets for the future and monitor these against actual achievements. Monthly accounts are also likely to be part of the workload. So, it is easy to see that management accountants are far more integrated and involved in a business than financial accountants.

Business types

A business can take many formats. It is important to understand these, as each may have different accounting requirements.

Sole trader

The simplest form of business is a sole trader. This is true of the typical self-employed person, like an electrician or plumber. As a sole trader, you are the only person who benefits from the rewards of the business. On the downside, you may also suffer all the losses.

Partnership

In a partnership two or more people come together and share the business rewards and risks. Partnerships are normally governed by a partnership agreement which sets out what each partner does, what share of profit they are entitled to, what risks they cover, etc. Partnerships are quite common in professions like accounting, law and medicine. This is mainly because no one person will have all the skills needed to operate the business successfully.

Limited company

Finally, a business may be a limited company. Unlike the previous two forms, the word limited suggests that the owners are somehow protected. The owners of a company are the shareholders. Their liability is limited to the amount they have unpaid on shares they agreed to buy. So, if I agreed to buy £10 of shares and I only paid £6, no matter what happens to the company, my liability is £4. In a sole trader or partnership, my liability could be unlimited and, in an extreme situation, I might have to sell personal assets to clear business debts.

Fundamental accounting terms

Before we progress to develop an understanding of the workings of book-keeping and accounting, there are some basic terms and concepts which need explaining.

Assets

An asset is something that is owned or something to which rights are available, which will deliver a benefit. Let me give you a simple example. Let's assume you start up your first business as a delivery service. You may have enough money to buy a delivery van, or you may not. You might lease a van to make deliveries and earn some money, that is, receive a benefit from the use of the van. So even though your business does not have the legal ownership of the van, it would be classified as an asset of the business. Of course, if you bought it outright, it would also be an asset.

Assets are often divided into non-current assets and current assets – we will see these terms again in later chapters. For now let's distinguish between them by looking at some examples. Non-current assets, as the name might suggest, are assets which tend to be a more long-term feature of the business. Typical examples would be business premises, a delivery van, machinery and office furniture. Current assets are more short-term in nature and typically refer to assets which are turned into cash within one year. Typical examples of current assets are the inventory of a business, money owed by customers and of course cash in the bank.

Liabilities

Now that you know what an asset is, a liability is simple to explain. You can think of it as the opposite of an asset – you must give away a benefit. In simple terms, you can consider a liability as a debt you owe someone. For example, if you buy goods from a supplier, you might get credit and not have to pay for 30 days. This debt would be a liability. Like assets, liabilities are classified as current and non-current. Current liabilities are normally repayable within one year, with non-current liabilities repayable after more than one year. Typical examples of current liabilities are amounts owed to suppliers, amounts owed to tax authorities and a bank overdraft. Examples of non-current liabilities would be a long-term bank loan or amounts owing on a lease (for the van we bought earlier!).

In other words

Assets are things you have and can use; **liabilities** are like claims on your business that you will have to pay.

Income and expenditure

Income is the money you receive from the sales of your goods or services. Income might also include items like bank interest you receive or income from investments. In Chapter 6, we will see how income is treated in the income statement.

Expenditure is what you would expect it to be: expenses incurred by the business. The key point here is that it must be expenditure for the business, and the business alone, to be classified as expenditure in an accounting sense. For example, the cost of a business trip to Rome is a business expense, but the cost of your spouse's shopping trip to Paris is not – even if the business paid for it.

Capital

You can think of capital as the money invested in a business by its owners. The make-up of capital depends on the type of business. If you are a sole trader or partnership, capital is the money personally invested in the business. For instance, maybe you got a redundancy payment and used it to start your own business. If a business is a limited company, then capital consists of the value of shares bought by shareholders of the company. In small, family-run companies, family members are typically the main shareholders as well as the management team. In the case of large companies, like Tesco or British Airways, shareholders may be individuals, banks or pension funds, and the management team is completely separate. The capital of a business also includes profits accumulated over time, a point I will return to in Chapters 5 and 6. Capital, like a liability, is also a claim on the business. It is effectively money owed to the business owner.

Fundamental accounting concepts

Now that you have an understanding of some basic terms, let's deal with some fundamental concepts in the world of accounting that apply no matter what type of business you have.

Business entity

In accounting, whether the business is a sole trader, partnership or company, the business is a separate entity. Let me give you an example. Assume you are a sole trader. Your delivery van breaks down so you get a mechanic to repair it. Your tumble dryer is not working too well and you learn that the mechanic is also quite handy at repairing appliances. The mechanic repairs both your van and tumble dryer. He gives you one bill for both repairs. Is the repair of the tumble dryer an expense of your business? You might have guessed no and you are correct. This is because the expense of the tumble dryer repair is not for the business entity even though you might think it is one and the same – as both are yours.

Each business entity needs to have separate sets of accounting records. If you have several businesses, each one may be a separate entity. Alternatively, many entities may fall under a single group which produces group accounts to give a complete picture of all business activities and entities.

Accruals concept

The accruals (or matching) concept is fundamental to the preparation of accounts for any business entity. It simply means that income and expenditure is accounted for when a transaction occurs, not when cash is paid. Here's an example. Your business prepares accounts to 31 December each year. You receive a bill from the electricity company on 5 January of the following year and this bill is paid on 23 January by direct debit. The bill relates to electricity consumed in December. So, under the accruals concept, the electricity cost would be accounted for in your accounts to 31 December. The cost relates to the period of the accounts and it does not matter when the bill is actually paid. Thus, your accounts to 31 December will show a liability for the unpaid bill.

In a similar way, let's assume you paid an insurance bill on 30 September. This bill covered the business insurance for one year from that date. Should the full cost be in your accounts to 31 December? If you said no, you are right. In this example, three months (1 October – 31 December) relate to the current year, and nine months to the next year. Thus, three months (or 25%) of the cost would appear in the current year accounts. The remaining (75%) is termed a prepayment and is classified as an asset. So, in summary, the accruals concept says that revenues should have associated costs matched against them, whether paid or not.

Going concern concept

This concept simply means that accounts are prepared under the assumption that the business will continue to operate for the foreseeable future. If the business discontinues, or is likely to, the value of some items might be affected. For example, if customers owed money, they might be reluctant to pay, or perhaps the value of the business premises might be higher or lower than the value in the accounts.

The accounting equation

The accounting (or balance sheet) equation is a simple rule which always applies in accounting. It is simply:

$$\text{Assets} - \text{Liabilities} = \text{Capital}$$

You already know what each of the three parts of the equation represent, so let's look at some examples.

First, you decide to start a business by placing £10,000 from your personal savings into a newly opened business bank account. The bank account is an asset of the business and the money you invest is the capital. Figure 1.1 shows how this can be depicted graphically.

FIGURE 1.1

| Assets £10,000 in bank | − | Liabilities Nil | = | Capital £10,000 you invested |

Both sides are equal, so the equation holds. Now you buy a computer and printer for your business which costs £1,000. This is of course a business asset. You pay for the computer from the bank account. Now, the equation looks like that in Figure 1.2.

FIGURE 1.2

You can see that the bank balance goes down, but you now have a new asset – your computer and printer. Both sides of the equation remain equal. Now, let's assume you buy some goods for resale, valued at £2,000, but you get 30 days' credit. No money leaves the bank account, but you now owe a supplier £2,000 – a liability. Also, you have acquired an asset – Inventory – to the value of £2,000. We can now portray the equation as in Figure 1.3. You can see that assets are now valued at £12,000, less liabilities of £2,000 leaving capital still at £10,000.

FIGURE 1.3

The accounting equation is effectively a portrayal of the balance sheet of a business, which we will examine in detail in Chapter 6. For now, it's enough to appreciate that this is one equation which will always apply. It can be rearranged of course, for example:

Assets = Capital + Liabilities

Sometimes people find it easier to remember this version and alter the wording a little to read something like:

Resources of the business = Resources given to the business
  (Assets)   (Capital + Liabilities)

You can choose which way to understand and remember it best.

Users of accounting information

As with any information, accounting information is produced with users of the information in mind. Who uses information generated by accounting and accountants? The main users are:

→ Managers and owners of a business – to make day-to-day decisions and to evaluate performance, for example, whether or not the business is profitable.

→ A prospective buyer of a business – any buyer would want information on the assets, liabilities and profits of a business.

→ A bank – if a business is to borrow money, a bank will want to see the existing liabilities and assess the ability to repay.

→ Tax authorities – they need to calculate tax on profits.

While all the above have different requirements, accounting information is a suitable compromise for all – it may not be perfect for everyone, but it is acceptable for most tasks.

Key points

→ Accounting collates and communicates business information.

→ There are two main branches of accounting; financial and management accounting.

→ Businesses may be sole traders, partnerships or a limited company.

→ An asset is something a business owns or has a right to; a liability, the opposite.

→ Capital is the money invested in a business by its owner.

→ Two fundamental accounting concepts are the accruals and going concern concepts. The former means the incomes and expenditures are matched against each other, the latter means the business is expected to continue to trade in the future.

→ The accounting equation always holds: Assets Liabilities = Capital.

The business plan

Chapter Two

Good fortune is what happens when opportunity meets with planning. THOMAS EDISON

It is important to have a business plan at the outset of a business venture. It may transpire that during the process of putting together a business plan you realise that things actually don't add up. Maybe the market is simply not there, or you cannot compete with cheap imports as your costs are just too high. Without a plan you're in the dark.

The basics of a business plan

A good business plan is something like a map in that it should help you to navigate to where you want to go. It is a necessity not just for you but also for potential investors or banks that may finance your business. A good business plan is a document in which you:

→ describe the nature of the business you wish to pursue;

→ examine the market for your goods/service and explain why there is a demand for what you will provide;

→ explain how you will exploit the market and achieve sales of your product or service;

→ show how the business is organised, and who will manage it;

→ demonstrate how you will produce and deliver the goods or services;

→ specify any assumptions on which financial projections are based;

→ make financial projections for income, expenditure, capital and cash requirements of the business.

As you can see, there is more to a business plan than financial data. The last two items are relevant for accounting and are the subject of this chapter.

Book-keeping and Accounts for Entrepreneurs

Know your costs

As part of a business plan, you must demonstrate a clear knowledge of the costs to make a product or to deliver a service and the ongoing running costs of the business. This may seem obvious, but it's not. On the BBC's *Dragons' Den* two entrepreneurs presented their business to the Dragons (who are among the UK's most successful entrepreneurs). The business was up and running for a while, supplying ethnic ready-meals to UK supermarkets. One of the Dragons, Duncan Bannatyne, quizzed them about the costs of the business. Within a few minutes it emerged that the cost of making each meal was approximately the same as the selling price. In other words, no money was left to pay expenses or make a profit. In a later episode, it was revealed that the business had ceased trading. This simple story shows the importance of knowing your costs. If you don't, there is a good chance your business won't survive

It is equally important that all relevant people in your business have some appreciation of costs. In their book, The *One Minute Entrepreneur*, Ken Blanchard and Don Hutson give a great example of a restaurant's chef who has a habit of regularly burning steaks. Each steak costs £6 and sells for £20. The restaurant owner tells the chef that the profit margin on each steak is 6 per cent of the selling price, i.e. £1.20. The chef quickly understands that each burnt steak (costing £6) requires five more to be sold (£1.20 × 5 – £6) to recoup the cost of the one he burned.

In other words

Profit margin is profit expressed as a percentage of selling price. Mark-up is profit as a percentage of cost price.

To help you understand costs in your business, let's see a number of ways costs can be classified.

Capital and revenue expenditure

The first important distinction to make is between costs (or expenditure) which are of a capital nature, compared to normal running costs.

Capital expenditure is expenditure on the purchase or modification of capital items, that is, non-current assets such as buildings, machinery or motor vehicles. Obviously, you need funds to purchase such items. We will see in Chapter 6 that capital expenditure usually is spread across several years in accounting, using an accounting technique known as depreciation.

Revenue expenditure (yes, I know, the term seems a bit of a contradiction) is expenditure which is incurred in the normal day-to-day running of a business. This includes items like telephone costs, fuel for a van or truck and wages. The table below demonstrates the difference between the two classifications, using the example of an executive limousine business.

Expenditure	Classification
Purchase of the limousine	Capital
Fitting bar and entertainment system in the limousine	Capital
Petrol costs	Revenue
Insurance	Revenue
Fees to local authority for licence to operate	Revenue
Rental of a garage to store limousine	Revenue
Cost of building a garage after a few months in business	Capital

Fixed and variable costs

Another way to classify costs is according to how they behave when the level of business output increases or decreases. As you might have guessed, a fixed cost is one which does not change, no matter what the business output. For instance, even if you sell absolutely nothing, you will still have to pay insurance costs for your business. Conversely, the more you sell, the lower your fixed cost per unit will be. For example, if you have fixed costs of £100,000 and produce and sell 10,000 units of your product, then the fixed cost for each item is £10. If you can sell 20,000 units the fixed cost per unit would be only £5. This might, of course, have an effect on your selling price.

A variable cost is one which increases or decreases in line with the business output. If you are manufacturing a product, the materials required for the product would be a variable cost. The more you produce, the greater the total material cost. If you produce nothing, the material cost would be nil.

The classification of costs as fixed or variable is not written in stone. Some costs may be a mixture of a fixed and variable element – for example, a utility bill (i.e. water, electricity) typically has a small fixed charge and a variable charge based on consumption. It is also often difficult to decide what is fixed or variable, and different businesses will classify things differently. However, when you have identified fixed and variable costs, you can do something very useful: find out how much you need to sell to break even.

Know your break-even point

Now that you know about different types of cost, consider Figure 2.1, which shows how you might calculate profit for your business.

FIGURE 2.1

How much is profit when a business breaks even? Nil is the correct answer, as 'break even' means a business makes neither a profit nor a loss. If profit is nil, then we can say if the business breaks even that sales less variable costs will equal fixed costs, as shown in Figure 2.2.

FIGURE 2.2

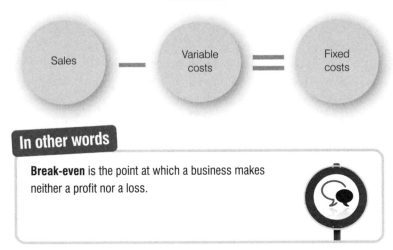

Break-even is the point at which a business makes neither a profit nor a loss.

Wouldn't it be useful to know how many units of product you need to sell to break even? This can be worked out quite easily, but first I need to introduce the term contribution.

Contribution

This is selling price less variable cost – the left-hand side of Figure 2.2. The greater the contribution, the more fixed costs are covered by sales, and hopefully a profit is made. It is possible to calculate a contribution for each unit of your product or service by taking the sales revenue of one unit and deducting the variable cost of one unit. With this in mind, I have modified Figure 2.2 a little, as portrayed in Figure 2.3.

FIGURE 2.3

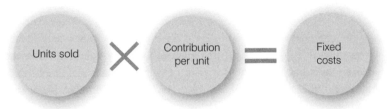

To break even, as shown in Figure 2.3, the units sold times the contribution per unit would equal fixed costs. Thus, if we want to calculate the units we need to sell to break even, we can rearrange Figure 2.3 as shown in Figure 2.4.

FIGURE 2.4

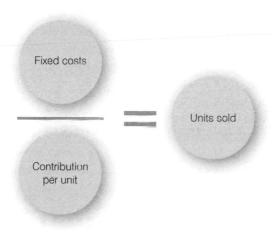

The formula in Figure 2.4 is very handy to know as it allows you to quickly estimate the volume of sales required to break even. Once you know the break-even sales volume, you can use it in your business plan and regard it as a target that is one you should achieve. You can also use the break-even concept for any business decision.

Basics of budgeting

The last point on the business plan checklist mentioned earlier was financial projections, or budgets. A budget is a financial plan for the future. Any business plan should at a minimum include a budget for income and expenditure (and thus profit). Some other budgets are also useful, in particular a cash budget. Let's look at how to prepare these budgets. The examples I use are slightly simplified, but should help you understand the concepts.

Budgeting for income

Before preparing a budget for income from sales for the first time, you need to work out a selling price. To do this, you need to know what it costs to produce your product or service. The costs would normally consist of costs of materials, labour and overhead. The first two costs are self-explanatory, but overhead requires some further explanation. Overhead cost is often termed an indirect cost. This is because such costs are not directly part of the product or service. For example, if I go into a bank to withdraw some cash, I go to a teller. This transaction has one direct cost, which is the cost of the teller's salary for the time taken to give me my cash. There are many indirect costs associated with this: the cost of light and heat in the bank, the bank manager's salary, cost of delivering cash to the bank, and so on.

You might have guessed from this example that allocating indirect costs to a product or service is not simple. You must make the effort, however. Some businesses will take direct costs and add a percentage to this figure to cover overhead. Others might divide overhead cost by the number of units they plan to produce/sell to get an overhead cost per unit. Once you have a unit cost for your product or service, you then add a desired profit mark-up to the cost to get the selling price. Of course this will also be influenced by other factors like what customers are willing to pay.

As most income from your business comes from sales of your product or service, the budget for sales is quite important. Once you have worked out your selling price, the sales budget is the first you should prepare. This is because what you sell determines the resources required to make your product or deliver your service. This in turn determines your costs for the period of the budget.

Assuming you have researched your market extensively, you should be able to determine two things: (1) how much you can sell, and, (2) at what price. The price may or may not be the price you want to achieve based on your initial selling-price calculations. However, with price and projected sales quantity on hand you can prepare a sales budget.

FIGURE 2.5

Sales budget

	Estimated sales units	Unit price £	Sales budget £
January	1,000	50	50,000
February	1,200	53	63,600
March	1,100	52	57,200
Total			**170,800**

You would normally prepare a budget for each month, as shown in Figure 2.5. A month is a useful base for comparison of your budget against what you actually sell. If corrective action is required, for instance if sales are lower than the target, you can react reasonably quickly to make up the shortfall.

Budgeting for expenditure

Once you know how much of your product or service you will supply, you can begin to create a budget for your expenditure. Combining the income and expenditure budget gives you a budgeted profit or loss. Let's look at how you might begin to plan your expenditure.

From your sales budget, you know how much you hope to sell. This is a good starting point for estimating your costs. Earlier, I outlined variable and fixed costs. Let's begin with variable costs, which change as your output changes. Let's use the example of a business manufacturing electronic components for the automotive industry. In such a business, the variable costs include the materials (printed circuits, chips etc.) from which the components are assembled and the costs of assembly (labour cost). Let's assume these two are the extent of the variable costs in the business. So, referring back to our knowledge of a sales budget, once we know what we hope to sell we can then prepare a budget for variable costs. Using the sales data in Figure 2.5, let's assume that our material cost per unit is £5 and each component takes two labour hours to assemble. Employees get paid £10 per hour. We can now prepare some budgeted costs as shown in Figure 2.6.

FIGURE 2.6

Variable costs budget

Month	Sales units	Material cost (× £5 per unit)	Labour cost (× 2 hrs × £10)
January	1,000	5,000	20,000
February	1,200	6,000	24,000
March	1,100	5,500	22,000

Simple enough! In your business, you may have many more costs, of course, but the basic concept is the same: start with your sales budget and then move on to look at costs which are related to (or driven by) what you sell. Now let's look at fixed costs, which are not driven by sales levels.

Fixed costs include things like insurance, salaries of managers, selling or administrative staff and perhaps advertising. The best (and easiest) method of budgeting for fixed costs is to estimate all such costs and try to place them in the correct month of your budget. For example, you could spread insurance costs and managers' salaries equally over a 12-month period, but you may have special advertising campaign expenses in a particular month. Try your best to as realistic as possible.

In Figure 2.7, I include both variable and fixed costs and sales to show a budget profit figure. I show three months purely for illustration purposes – I would suggest you prepare a budget for at least one year.

FIGURE 2.7

Budgeted income and expenditure

	January £	February £	March £	Total £
Sales	50,000	63,600	57,200	170,800
Variable costs				
Materials	(5,000)	(6,000)	(5,500)	(16,500)
Labour	(20,000)	(24,000)	(22,000)	(66,000)
	(25,000)	(30,000)	(27,500)	(82,500)
Contribution	25,000	33,600	29,700	88,300
Fixed costs				
Salaries	(5,000)	(5,000)	(5,000)	(15,000)
Insurance	(1,000)	(1,000)	(1,000)	(3,000)
Advertising		(6,000)		(6,000)
	(6,000)	(12,000)	(6,000)	(24,000)
Budgeted profit	19,000	21,600	23,700	64,300

How you present your budget is up to you. Figures 2.5 to 2.7 are just examples. In Figure 2.7 for instance, I include contribution in my presentation, but this is not necessary. You might also decide to show just one figure for fixed costs, with a supporting analysis attached. Or you might not bother to distinguish between fixed and variable costs at all. But, whatever approach you take, be sure you get all your revenues and costs in your budget and provide some form of summary like Figure 2.7.

Budgeting for capital expenditure

As you know, capital expenditure relates to the purchase of items of a capital nature – delivery trucks, machinery, etc. It is important also to have a budget for capital expenditure for two reasons. First, it will help form a basis for a budget for assets and liabilities, and, second, it allows you to estimate how much cash is required – which is important for a cash budget.

When budgeting for capital expenditure, the easiest thing to do is to estimate the amount you will spend and when. This information can then be used as inputs to a cash budget and also as a budgeted expenditure in the form of depreciation. (Depreciation, as mentioned earlier, is the technique used to spread the cost of capital expenditure over several years.) In Chapter 3, I will discuss how a business can raise finance for capital items, but for now let's proceed to the cash budget to see how capital expenditure affects this.

Cash budget

The ability of a business to generate cash is very important. Cash is normally generated from sales of a product or service, but might also include things like sales of assets or the issue of shares (if a limited company). If you cannot generate cash, you will run into all sorts of problems – you cannot pay suppliers or wages, for example. Chapters 8 and 9 will provide much more detail on the importance of cash.

Let's use Figure 2.7 as a starting point. To prepare a cash budget, we need some further information, which is given overleaf:

→ All sales are on credit. Customers pay the month following sale.

→ Material suppliers are paid one month in arrears.

→ Labour costs and all fixed costs are paid in the month incurred.

→ Some office equipment will be bought in February for £5,000 and a delivery van in March for £15,000.

→ You invest £20,000 of your own money in the business in January.

The key points about the cash budget relate to when cash is actually paid. I am assuming this is a brand new business and thus the bank account will have no funds in it. Figure 2.9 shows the cash budget.

FIGURE 2.8

Cash budget

	January £	*February* £	*March* £
Cash receipts			
Sales		50,000	63,600
Capital	20,000		
Total receipts	20,000	50,000	63,600
Cash payments			
Materials		(5,000)	(6,000)
Labour	(20,000)	(24,000)	(22,000)
Fixed costs	(6,000)	(12,000)	(6,000)
Office equipment		(5,000)	
Delivery van			(15,000)
Total payments	(26,000)	(46,000)	(49,000)
Net cash in/(out)	(6,000)	4,000	14,600
Opening cash	0	(6,000)	(2,000)
Closing cash	(6,000)	(2,000)	12,600

Let me explain some items very briefly. Cash from sales is received one month after the sale, hence the £50,000 cash receipt in February relates to January sales and so on. Similarly, material suppliers are paid one month after sale, so the £5,000 paid in February relates to materials bought in January. All other cash receipts and payments are in the month incurred. I also show a figure each month for 'net cash in/(out)'. This is simply the cash receipts minus the cash paid in a month. There was no money in the business bank account to begin with (the business had just started) thus the opening cash is nil. Each month I have added the opening cash to the net cash in/out to calculate the closing cash. The closing cash for January becomes the opening cash for February and so on.

Can you see anything wrong with the cash budget above? If you do, jot it down here:

_____

_____

_____

I hope you spotted that we have a negative closing cash of £6,000 in January and a negative £2,000 in February. What does this mean? It simply means that if nothing is done, the business will be short of cash It will not be able to pay all the labour and fixed costs in January, for example.

The cash budget above is not wrong – it's based on the information we have – but it does highlight a problem. So what can be done? There are typically three ways to resolve such a problem: (1) get cash in earlier – perhaps from customers; (2) postpone paying suppliers or other expenditure; (3) obtain additional cash – perhaps a temporary overdraft. I am going to choose option 2 and assume that it is possible to pay for fixed costs one month later rather than immediately. Now the cash budget would look like that in Figure 2.9.

Alternatively, the business could increase the initial investment to £26,000 or seek a bank overdraft to cover the cash shortfall. Whatever the method used to resolve a cash shortfall, the preparation of the cash budget highlights the problem and gives time to find a solution. That's certainly better than running out of cash! This example also demonstrates the fact that budgets may have a number of drafts before a final version is derived.

The business plan

FIGURE 2.9

Cash budget

	January £	February £	March £
Cash receipts			
Sales		50,000	63,600
Capital	20,000		
Total receipts	20,000	50,000	63,600
Cash payments			
Materials		(5,000)	(6,000)
Labour	(20,000)	(24,000)	(22,000)
Fixed costs		(6,000)	(12,000)
Office equipment		(5,000)	
Delivery van			(15,000)
Total payments	(20,000)	(40,000)	(55,000)
Net cash in/(out)	0	10,000	8,600
Opening cash	0	0	10,000
Closing cash	0	10,000	18,600

Budget assumptions

One of the most important issues to consider when preparing any budget is the validity of the underlying assumptions used. For example, when preparing the cash budget above, I assumed customers will pay in one month. What if they don't? Or similarly, what if the advertising cost used earlier doubled to £12,000? Or if you fail to achieve the budgeted sales price due to increased competition? As we cannot look to the future with 100 per cent certainty, all budgets are based on assumptions.

Advantages of budgets

Although budgets can never be totally accurate and are based on many assumptions, they do offer quite a number of advantages for a business. Budgets force a business to think about the future, or, in other words, to plan. I have thus far considered a budget solely as part of a business plan. Once your business is up and running, budgets are prepared on a more regular basis. As a business grows, the budget preparation process can become quite a formal exercise conducted on an annual or more frequent basis. Preparing budgets helps a business to think about what resources are necessary to achieve its aims and to plan accordingly, to ensure the required resources are available – including cash, materials and people.

Budgets, particularly in larger enterprises, also help co-ordinate the activities of the business. For example, it would be pointless if a sales budget prepared by the sales manager had a volume of goods too high for the production manager to produce in the factory. A consequence of the co-ordination is improved communication between sections of a business.

A budget is also a target to achieve and thus may be a motivating factor for managers or other members of a business. Quite often, a business will pay bonuses to managers based on their performance against budget. It may also, of course, be a de-motivating factor if the target was too hard to achieve!

Web bonus

At our website, **www.forentrepreneursbooks.com**, click on the 'Book-keeping and Accounting for Entrepreneurs' button. On the link for Chapter 2 you'll find a sample business plan and some useful spreadsheet templates to help you prepare your budgets.

Key points

→ Accounting numbers are an important component of a business plan.

→ 'Break even' is a useful concept to help make business decisions. It is a useful target to achieve.

→ Budgeting is an essential part of planning for the future of a business. Budgets should be prepared for income and expenditure, capital expenditure, and cash.

Next steps

What are the fixed and variable costs of your business? What is your break-even sales volume?

If you're starting out in business, prepare a budget as part of the business plan. When will you have it complete?

_____

_____

_____

_____

Financing your business

Chapter Three

If you are a first-time entrepreneur, it will not be easy to obtain finance and you will most likely have to put your hands in your own pocket. Financing must be part of your business plan – and you need a business plan to approach any person or institution for finance. Think about the sources of finance mentioned in this chapter and find one or more which suits your business. Consider the costs of each finance source and any conditions attached. You will have to do the footwork – finance will not just fall on your doorstep! But it will be worth the effort to see your fledgling business grow.

Finance for a first-time entrepreneur

Generally, a business has two main types of financing need:

→ Finance for investment, expansion and growth.
→ Finance for the day-to-day activities of the business – often termed working capital.

FIGURE 3.1

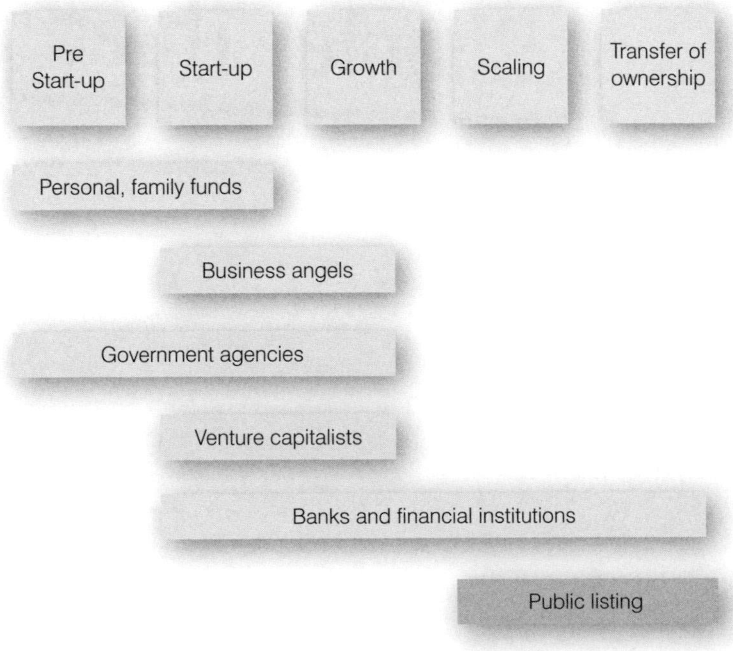

Pre Start-up	Start-up	Growth	Scaling	Transfer of ownership

Personal, family funds

Business angels

Government agencies

Venture capitalists

Banks and financial institutions

Public listing

A start-up business will need finance for both investment and working capital. Any finance provider (for example, a bank) will examine the risks associated with the business plan, and if it is deemed too risky, will not provide finance. It is quite common for finance for first-time entrepreneurs to come from a combination of sources, thereby enabling the risk to be spread. Figure 3.1 illustrates the finance sources available to businesses at various stages of development – the latter stages will be described in more detail later in the chapter.

Personally financing the business

Often, a start-up business is financed by personal funds. Personal loans, credit cards or savings are frequently used, maybe even a redundancy payment. If you have done your homework and have a good business plan, you may feel confident about putting in your own money. If you are like me, you might feel this is a bit too risky. The alternative obviously is to seek finance from other sources. I would suggest you try to get finance from wherever you can, but be under no illusions, as you will have to contribute at least some finance yourself. If you decide to be a sole trader, this means lodging your funds in a separate business bank account. If you decide to be a limited company, you will have to buy shares in the company and lodge the cash payment for shares in a company bank account.

Business angels

A 'business angel' is a private individual who invests capital in an early-stage business and may also contribute know-how or experience to its operation and development. Such finance is an alternative to bank financing or venture capital, neither of which may be available to the business at that point. It's common for business angels to form networks in an effort to match those seeking finance with those who have some cash to invest. Your business may have to be a limited company to obtain this type of finance so that the business angels can easily take partial ownership by buying shares in the company.

Government agencies

Both central and local government agencies often provide funding for small and start-up businesses. There may be a lot of red tape involved in getting government funding, but you should not write it off as a potential source. The location of your business may play a major role, as frequently local or central government have policies to regenerate localities, which means businesses are needed to provide employment. Available funding in such 'assisted' areas may be broader and of higher value than in other locations.

Typically, government funding is available under the following headings:

→ Research and development – support for new research is more likely to be available,

→ Employment and training – where, for example, training is provided by a government agency at low cost, or an employee's wage cost is covered,

→ Environmental grants – funds may be available for business to adopt 'green' ways of working; such amounts may be small,

→ Capital investment – governments may provide assistance to businesses to acquire capital equipment. Such incentives can be attractive and are normally available where certain government policy aims are being supported – for example, inner-city development or safeguarding local jobs.

Finance from government agencies may or may not be repayable. In most instances, it is not repayable, hence you may have quite a complicated and stringent vetting procedure. But the effort can be worth it.

In addition, government assistance (as opposed to funding) may be available. In the UK the government offers guarantees to commercial banks that loan to small business. The scheme, called the Small Firms Loan Guarantee, provides the lender with a 75 per cent guarantee on the loan amount. The borrower must pay a small percentage of the loan as a fee for the guarantee. Such a scheme allows banks to be more open and flexible towards small business.

Time saver

Get in touch with your local business organisation, for instance a Chamber of Commerce. They often have lots of information on how government agencies can help entrepreneurs.

Venture capitalists

Venture capitalists are similar to the business angels I mentioned earlier. They provide funds to limited companies at the early stages of development. The difference with venture capitalists is that they normally pool their resources into venture capital funds or a dedicated investment firm. Venture capitalists may be institutional investors (banks) or high-net-worth individuals. Venture capitalists also often bring managerial and technical expertise to a business.

Banks and financial institutions

Banks and other financial institutions are in the business of providing finance to what they term 'creditworthy projects', which are normally backed by assets. Most banks will give unsecured finance for a small amount of money (perhaps £5,000–£10,000) to entrepreneurs and more (perhaps £10,000–£15,000) to established businesses.

Beyond this amount, banks will typically seek security of some form. They perceive new and developing businesses as higher risk and thus, beyond these amounts, often require security on a specific asset (an office building, for example), or a personal guarantee. However, many businesses, particularly those in the early stages of development and those in the services sector, have few or no assets to provide as security against a bank loan. So what can banks actually do for your business? Here are some options:

→ A bank overdraft – this is a facility on the business bank account to draw funds to an agreed level. If your business is a limited company, you as a company director may be required to give a personal guarantee, as this provides more security to the bank, particularly in the case of a new company.

→ A business loan – a business loan is normally repayable over a number of years, maybe three or five. It is likely that security will be required.

→ Leasing – a lease agreement is when a bank effectively buys an asset and the business gets the benefits (and suffers the costs) of ownership. Payments are made at regular intervals, usually monthly, to the bank. Ownership transfers to the business once all payments are made. Leasing is often used to fund the purchase of motor vehicles or other equipment.

Danger!

As I am sure you know, banks will charge interest for all finance, so shop around for the best deal. Also, if your business is new, be absolutely sure to have a business plan prepared (see Chapter 2) before you go to a bank seeking finance.

Financing working capital

Working capital is an accounting term which means the value of current assets less the value of current liabilities. Let me remind you of the meaning of each term. Current assets are assets held in the short term. Typical examples are cash, inventories and amounts due from customers (trade receivables). Current liabilities are liabilities which a business will settle with 12 months. Examples are amounts owing to suppliers (trade payables), a bank overdraft, or amounts owing to tax authorities.

Let's think a little more about some of the elements of working capital, namely inventories (stocks), trade receivables and trade payables. You may not realise it initially, but each of these is either consuming or holding cash. Thus, prudent management of each is a good idea. I will explain each in a little more detail.

Inventories

Inventories have an obvious value – the purchase price. What happens if you hold on to inventory for too long or have too much? The answer is twofold. First, it can decrease in value or become obsolete. Second, inventory is unsold product in which cash is invested. The more inventory held, and the longer the holding period, the more cash is tied up, which could be used for something else. High-street department stores, for example, often have summer or winter sales. These sales fulfil two functions. End-of-season stock can be sold off at a lower price, as to hold it runs the risk of the value falling even lower. Holding the stock until the next season also means cash is tied up. The key is to get the balance right between holding stock and not having too much cash invested in stock. There is no magic-bullet answer to this problem. If you don't hold enough stock, you might lose sales; if you hold too much, your cash is tied up. Experience, a good stock-control system and good supplier relationships (maybe they can hold the stock) will all help you solve this issue. Of course, if you are a service business, you will have less (or no) problems with inventory.

Trade receivables

Trade receivables arise when you sell on credit. Selling on credit is normal, especially if you want to sell to other businesses. Like inventories, cash is tied up in trade receivables. There are two things you need to consider: (1) who to give credit to, and (2) how much credit to give for how long. Who to give credit to should be based on some form of vetting procedure. You can use what is termed the 'five Cs of credit' as a guideline:

→ **Capital.** The customer must appear financially sound – in Chapter 9, you will learn how to analyse accounts to help you determine the financial state of a business.

→ **Capacity.** This is the capacity to repay. You should seek credit references from your potential customer.

→ **Collateral.** Can any security be taken? For example, can you retain title on the goods until they are fully paid for?

→ **Conditions.** What are the current economic or industry conditions? This can influence the ability to repay.

→ **Character.** Is it possible to assess the honesty and integrity of the business and its management?

How much credit is given will be determined by how risky you think the potential customer is. You could ask the referees how much credit they give. How long you give the credit for is often best gauged by what the industry or sector standard is (maybe 30 or 60 days), or, perhaps, by the bargaining power of the customer. Other factors to consider are the risk of non-payment and the level of competition.

Danger!

Keep track of how much money your customers owe you. Invoice them promptly and once they exceed the period of credit granted, start chasing them (politely, of course) for payment.

Trade payables

Trade payables are the amount you owe to suppliers. As a start-up business you may find it difficult to get credit. Quite often suppliers will ask for immediate cash payment (called cash with order). After a while, as you build up a reputation with a supplier, they will grant you credit. Once you get credit, paying on time is a good idea. Otherwise your credit rating will be affected.

The bottom line on financing working capital

So what does all this mean for the financing of your business? Put simply, if there is a time gap between when you need to pay your supplier and when you get paid from your customer, how do you fill this finance gap? The first thing is to try to keep this gap as small as possible. For instance, try to collect cash as quickly as you can from customers. Second, you may invest some cash in the business at the outset to fund this gap. Finally, you might seek a bank overdraft. The most important thing is not to forget finance for working capital in your business plan and budget projections.

Danger!

It is possible for a business to 'overtrade', which means increasing sales without corresponding increases in working capital, such as inventories. So 'cut your coat according to your cloth'.

Financing as the business grows

As your business grows, all the sources of finance I have described are still relevant. As your reputation grows, and hopefully your profits in tandem, you will find it easier to deal with banks in particular. This is because your asset base and income will have improved over time, providing more security and repayment capacity from the bank's view.

Finance for growing your business: going public

The most obvious source of finance for growing your business is the business profits. As profits are made, business owners may elect not to withdraw all profits, but rather leave some in the business to invest in the future. Retained profits are a cheap source of finance. However, as shown in Figure 3.1, it is also possible to raise finance through a public listing of a limited company. Normally, companies start as private limited companies. Although all companies have shares, private companies cannot sell shares to the general public. Shares sold to the public, which would of course include investors, are normally sold through a stock market like the London or New York stock exchanges. To sell shares on a stock exchange a company must become a public company.

Converting from a private to a public company is not a simple process. Under UK law, a public company must have a minimum issued share capital of £50,000 and obtain a trading certificate confirming this fact from Companies House. In addition, a public company must seek permission from the Financial Services Authority to trade its shares on the stock market. The offer for sale of shares is contained in a document called a prospectus. This is a long and complicated document containing information on the financial status of the company, details on the company's operations, details of the share issue (price and number of shares), application procedures to purchase shares, and much more. The process of becoming a public company will also involve the services of accountants, lawyers and banks. As you might guess, the process is not cheap. For example, a UK accounting firm, UHY Hacker Young, reported in 2007 that the cost of a public listing on the Alternative Investment Market (AIM) of the London Stock Exchange was approximately 18 per cent of the funds raised (where the funds raised range from £2 million to £10 million).

Despite the cost, successful private companies seek a public listing for one simple reason: the access to finance is dramatically increased. The number of business ventures which progress from start-up to public listing is likely to be quite small. But it does happen, and when it does it can provide access to vast amounts of finance. Continued access will depend on how successful a company is. If your company is lucky enough to make it to a public listing, you won't need this book any more – you'll be surrounded by lots of professional advisors!

Key points

→ A business needs sufficient finance to start up and continue to grow. For a new business, often finance from personal sources is needed.

→ There are a number of sources of finance for a start-up business: banks, business angels, venture capitalists and government agencies. You will most likely have to contribute some finance out of personal resources.

→ Ensure you understand the elements of working capital and the need to finance it.

Next step

What sources of finance are available to your business? Find out and note them below. Which sources are most suited to your business?

_____

_____

_____

_____

Keeping the records and preparing accounts

Part Two

'Keeping the books'

Chapter Four

In this chapter, I introduce what is commonly referred to as 'keeping the books'. As you trade, the detail of each business transaction needs to be captured and recorded somewhere. This captured information is the basis for the preparation of a set of accounts (financial statements) for a business. The chapter describes how business transactions are recorded in a manual format. Once you know how this works you may want to use a software package which can make more efficient use of your time. I give an example of one such package towards the end of this chapter.

The books of prime entry (day books)

As this rather official title suggests, the books of prime entry are the 'books' where business transactions are first recorded from source documents like invoices and cheques. The term 'day books' is a more common term and is the one I like to use. They are called day books as, in a manual book-keeping system, each type of business transaction would have a separate hardback type book where the records are written each day. Such books are still available to buy in any good office supply store. They are usually called 'analysis books'.

In other words

The **books of prime entry** are the first place that business transactions are recorded in a business. They may be a 'book', or, more commonly now, accounting software.

The following sections give examples of what each of the day books looks like. The most common day books are:

→ sales day book – which records credit sales;

→ purchases day book – which records credit purchases;

→ cash receipts book – which records cash received from customers and other sources;

→ cheque payments book – which records payments made by cheque/debit from the business bank account;

→ petty cash book – which records minor cash expenses;

→ general journal – which records any other transaction not captured in other day books.

The data for each day book comes from various 'source documents', like sales invoices, suppliers' invoices or cheque books.

The VAT factor

Tax authorities like to see good records in a business. Taxation, particularly Value-Added Tax (VAT), is something which a business may need to collect on behalf of the tax authorities. Normally, there is a turnover (sales) threshold above which a business must register for VAT (currently £67,000 in the UK). Assuming your turnover will be above such a threshold, this raises two requirements for your business: (1) you need to capture any VAT in a business transaction and record it separately, and (2) if you don't keep good records from day one, you might find yourself very quickly having problems. I am at pains to emphasise these two points as I have seen a number of businesses run into trouble. One business did not bother to register for VAT initially and ended up with a £300,000 liability within 12 months. For convenience, the day books I describe below assume the business is registered for VAT. If not, you just leave out any columns labelled 'VAT'.

Use spreadsheets for your day books instead of analysis books. It saves quite a lot of time adding up numbers.

Sales day book

The sales day book records sales made on credit to your customers. Sales invoices are the source documents for this day book. It is likely that credit sales will comprise the majority of your sales, unless you are in a retail business. Figure 4.1 shows a sales invoice from the business of Trilby Traders to John Adams (both fictitious names).

FIGURE 4.1

	Invoice	Inv No: 134
Trilby Traders		20-Oct-08
123 High St,		
Anytown		
Invoice to:		
John Adams		
80 Low St,		
Othertown		
		£
Goods		1,000
Vat @ 15%		150
Invoice total		1,150

Sales invoicing

You can prepare sales invoices in many ways. Some businesses often start with simple pre-printed duplicate invoice books. You could also type invoices in Microsoft Word. Whatever your method, ensure your invoices have some form of sequence number and keep a copy of every invoice.

Let's see how this invoice would be recorded in the sales day book of Trilby Traders. All we need do is take the information from the invoice and place it in the correct columns. Figure 4.2 shows the sales day book with the invoice to John Adams recorded.

FIGURE 4.2

Trilby Traders

Sales day book

Date		Ref.	Total (£)	Sales (£) 15%	Sales (£) 25%	VAT (£)
20/10/2008	John Adams	134	1,150	1,000		150
			1,150	1,000		150

The sales day book shows a number of columns. The first three reflect the date, customer and invoice number from Figure 4.1. The total column is simply the invoice total, which includes VAT. The next two columns (Sales 15%, Sales 25%) show the net of VAT invoice amount. In the case of the invoice to John Adams, the applicable VAT rate was 15 per cent. The VAT amount (i.e. £150) is shown under the VAT column. Why separate columns for sales at each VAT rate? Well, a return of VAT must be made to the taxation authorities at regular intervals (bimonthly or quarterly, for instance). In each return you must report your sales at each VAT rate. If you capture this in the sales day book, you save yourself a lot of work later. Also, VAT is not relevant to the preparation of financial statements (see Chapter 6) as a business only collects VAT on behalf of the taxation authorities.

Figure 4.3 shows some more invoices I have created and recorded in the sales day book. Each invoice is recorded in a similar manner to the first example. You will notice the net amount of each invoice is recorded under a column depending on the rate of VAT on the invoice.

FIGURE 4.3

Trilby Traders

Sales day book

Date		Ref.	Total (£)	Sales (£) 15%	Sales (£) 25%	VAT (£)
20/10/2008	John Adams	134	1,150	1,000		150
21/10/2008	James O'Toole	135	375		300	75
22/10/2008	Mary Carpenter	136	50		40	10
23/10/2008	Fred Smith	137	2,500		2,000	500
23/10/2008	Joseph Hunt	138	1,250		1,000	250
24/10/2008	Edward Henry	139	345	300		45
31/10/2008	John Adams	140	(115)	(100)		(15)
			5,555	1,200	3,340	1,015

You might have also noticed that the transaction for John Adams on 31 October (in Figure 4.3) is shown as a minus figure. This means that a credit note was issued to him, perhaps for goods returned by him. Traditionally, goods returned by customers are entered in a sales returns day book, which would have a very similar layout to a sales day book. In practice, recording a return in the manner depicted in Figure 4.3 is acceptable unless you specifically want to be able to identify returns. You might want to do this if returns are of a high value or occur quite often. Tracking returns in detail may help you identify underlying problems with your product. If you are a service business, returns are irrelevant but you still might need to issue credit notes to customers, for instance if you overcharged a customer in error.

Purchases day book

The purchases day book records purchases made on credit from suppliers. Suppliers provide your business with materials and/or services. The source documents for the purchases day books are suppliers' invoices. The layout of a purchases day book is similar to that of the sales day book. Figure 4.4 shows the purchases day book for Trilby Traders. I have again created some examples.

FIGURE 4.4

Trilby Traders

Purchases day book

Date		Ref.	Total (£)	Purchases (£) 15%	Purchases (£) 25%	VAT (£)
15/10/2008	Mark Hanley	300	575	500		75
16/10/2008	John's Parts	301	175		140	35
17/10/2008	Town Council – water charge	302	50		40	10
20/10/2008	AB Supplies Ltd	303	700		560	140
23/10/2008	MegaSupplies	304	875		700	175
25/10/2008	AB Supplies Ltd	305	(230)	(200)		(30)
29/10/2008	John's Parts	306	230	200		30
			2,375	500	1,440	435

There are a few differences from the sales day book. The reference column has a different number sequence. I also show a credit note from a supplier (AB Supplies Ltd) as a minus figure in the purchases day book. This could also be shown in a separate purchases returns day book.

Time saver

Keep suppliers' invoices filed in a folder using some form of sequential number. I often simply label the first supplier invoice in a business with the number 1 and go from there. Once the sequence number is recorded in the purchases day book you can easily find it in your files.

Cash receipts book

The cash receipts book records cash received by the business. Generally, cash will be lodged to the business bank account. The sources of cash for a business would typically fall into three categories:

1 cash sales;

2 cash received from customers you sold to on credit;

3 other cash received.

Cash sales are sales made to customers who are not given credit. For example, a building supplies business will normally have cash sales to the general public and credit sales to building contractors. Other cash received might include items like money received from the sale of an asset, or bank interest.

The layout of the cash receipts book is shown in Figure 4.5. The source documents for the cash book could be cheques or remittance advices received from customers, or cash register rolls.

FIGURE 4.5

Trilby Traders

Cash receipts book

Date		Ref.	Total (£)	Debtors (£)	Sales (£) 15%	Sales (£) 25%	Misc. (£)	VAT (£)	Lodged (£)
01/10/2008	Cash sales		115		100			15	
02/10/2008	John Adams	456	2,000	2,000					2,115
06/10/2008	Cash sales	457	125			100		25	125
25/10/2008	James O'Toole	458	375	375					375
31/10/2008	Mary Carpenter		50	50					
31/10/2008	Refund of water charges	459	10				10		60
			2,675	2,425	100	100	10	40	2,675

A date, description, reference and total column is shown, as in the sales and purchases day books. After this, things are a little different. I show columns depicting cash receipts from three sources: payments from customers sold to on credit, cash sales, and miscellaneous. The column labelled 'Debtors' shows receipts from customers (debtors) who have been granted credit. The next two columns show cash sales at the relevant VAT rate. The VAT amount associated with the cash sale is shown in the VAT column. See, for example, the cash sale dated 1 October. The column labelled 'Misc' shows cash receipts from miscellaneous sources – a refund of water charges in the example. Finally, there is a column labelled 'Lodged'. This column shows amounts lodged to the business bank account. Looking at Figure 4.5, you will see an amount of £2,115 lodged on 2 October. This amount is made up of the cash sales from 1 October of £115 and a receipt from John Adams on 2 October of £2,000. As you can imagine, many cash receipts are often grouped together in one lodgement for the bank. The lodgement on 2 October is an example of this. The reference number 456 in the reference column refers to the lodgement in some way, most likely to a slip in a pre-printed lodgement book your bank has given you.

Time saver

Keep a record of the make-up of each lodgement. Lots of small businesses I know photocopy cheques from customers, staple them together and write the lodgement reference on the first page. Also, check your bank statement periodically (or do this online if you have the facility) to see if a customer has paid direct to the bank account.

Cheque payments book

The cheque payments book records payments made from the business bank account. Cheques may not be the only method used to make payments from your business bank account. Direct debits, standing orders and other forms of electronic payments may be more common. The source document for the cheque payments will vary. If you use a cheque book, the stub of the cheque book will be one source. If you use direct debits and/or standing orders you might know the amount in advance and record it. If you use internet banking you might record the transaction as you complete it. You can also use the bank statements to find payments which you might not have recorded in the cheque payments book. No matter the form or source, all payments from the business bank account are recorded in the cheque payments book. Figure 4.6 shows the cheque payments book for Trilby Traders, with some examples.

FIGURE 4.6

Trilby Traders

Cheque payments book

Date		Chq ref.	Total (£)	Creditors (£)	Light & heat (£)	Wages (£)	Phone (£)	VAT (£)	Misc. (£)
03/10/2008	AB Supplies Ltd	500789	340	340					
06/10/2008	Electricity company	500790	130		130				
07/10/2008	Staff wages	500791	500			500			
08/10/2008	Telephone company	DD	120				120		
18/10/2008	Hill Motors – new van	DD	5,000						5,000
23/10/2008	Taxation authorities	DD	300					300	
31/10/2008	Petty cash	500792	10						10
			6,400	340	130	500	120	300	5,010

The layout of a cheque payments book will vary from business to business. The example in Figure 4.6 shows the date and narrative columns – similar to the other day books. The reference column shows the cheque number or other reference, for instance DD for direct debit. Next is a total column followed by a number of analysis columns. The 'Creditors' column shows amounts paid to suppliers. Other columns show the type of expense for each payment – light and heat, wages, phone and miscellaneous. The cheque for petty cash in the miscellaneous column is explained in the next section. The VAT column in this example actually shows a payment of VAT to the taxation authorities. This represents the periodic payment of VAT collected by the business to the authorities. I explain this in more detail later in the chapter.

Petty cash book

Some businesses keep a petty cash book. This day book records minor cash expenses such as payment for tea or coffee for the office. Figure 4.7 shows an example of how a petty cash book might look for Trilby Traders.

FIGURE 4.7

Trilby Traders

Petty cash book

Date		Paid out		Date		Vch. ref.	Total (£)	Teas (£)	Cleaner (£)	Office Supplies (£)
01/10/2008	Balance	100.00		03/10/08	Tea	234	1.39	1.39		
31/10/2008	Cheque		10.09	06/10/08	Window cleaner	235	5.50		5.50	
				07/10/08	Pens	236	3.20			3.20
					Total spend		10.09	1.39	5.50	3.20
				31/10/08	Balance		100.00			
		110.09					110.09			

The example shows a somewhat familiar layout. This time, however, there are two 'sides' to the book. A petty cash book normally uses what is called the imprest system. This simply means that a certain petty cash balance is maintained and topped up. In Figure 4.7, the first three columns show that on 1 October, the opening balance of petty cash is £100. This usually represents actual cash held in a cash box. The remaining columns show the petty cash expenses, analysed by expense type. Each expense item is usually recorded on a petty cash voucher (you can buy these at any office supplies store) and a receipt is attached. The expenses are then totalled – £10.09 in the example. A cheque for this amount is cashed – look back at Figure 4.6 and you can see one for £10 (I have ignored the pennies). The cash paid in replenishes the petty cash balance to £100.

You might be thinking this is a lot of effort for such a small amount of money. I agree! However, there may be instances where not keeping some form of petty cash system could create problems for you. Any cash payments to employees could be deemed as income and thus taxable, for example. Some years ago I had to create a petty cash book for a small haulage business. In this case, drivers were often on longer trips and needed money for meals or overnight accommodation. The amounts were small and did not warrant drivers having credit cards, so they were given cash. Following a tax inspection, the business had to use a petty cash system for the drivers' expenses as the tax inspectors were not happy with cash being paid to employees without any supporting records. However, in my view, unless the amounts of petty cash are increasing or consistently paid to employees, I think you might not need to worry too much about this day book.

General journal

This is the last of the day books. A general journal (or journal for short) is a simple book which records a transaction that cannot be recorded in any other day book. The journal is more often used by accountants, but it can prove useful to record errors made in other day books. Figure 4.8 shows a sample journal.

FIGURE 4.8

Trilby Traders

Journal

Date	Account	Debit (£)	Credit (£)
31/10/2008	Bad debts	345	
	Edward Henry		345
	(customer bankrupt)		

The journal is basic in appearance – simply date, narrative and debit and credit columns. Don't worry about the meaning of debit and credit for now – Chapter 5 will deal with this. In the example, I show how a bad customer debt (that is, a debt that will not be paid) is recorded. A bad debt cannot be recorded in the sales or sales returns day books, so we must include it in the journal. The most important thing about a journal is putting some comment about the transaction so that you (and others) can trace it in the future.

Payroll and VAT

Your business may have some employees. If so, then you must maintain payroll (wages) records. The easiest thing to do is use payroll software.

Sage and Quickbooks provide UK payroll software cheaply. Such software is also available for other countries. If you search the internet you might also find some free software. Once you use software, the only additional recording you have to do is the hours worked by employees. I would strongly advise you to use software, as the taxation and social insurance arrangements can be quite awkward to get to terms with in a manual system. For instance, any taxes or social insurance deducted from employees is paid over periodically (usually monthly) to the tax authorities.

In the example cheque payments book (Figure 4.6), I showed a payment of VAT being made to the tax authorities. Let me explain this a little more. If you are registered for VAT, you are effectively a tax collector for the government. Thus, you have to make returns to the VAT authorities detailing VAT you have charged on sales and VAT you have been charged by suppliers. The return is made periodically, typically every two, three or six months. The data for the return comes from the day books. Let's use the sales and purchases day books as an example. In Figure 4.3, the total VAT charged to customers is £1,015 – the total of the VAT column. The VAT charged by suppliers is £435 (see Figure 4.4). The amount of VAT charged by suppliers can be deducted from what was charged to customers. The net amount, £580, is paid to the tax authorities. In the cheque payments book (see Figure 4.6), the payment is £300, which we will assume was payment of VAT from a previous month. Thus, Trilby Traders has a liability to pay £580. It is possible for a business to have a refund of VAT, too, where the total VAT amounts charged by suppliers is greater than the amount charged on sales.

Book-keeping: some practical guidelines

Now for a few practical pointers in the book-keeping area. During my years as an accountant I have developed a few simple guidelines which ultimately make life a little easier. Some should also contribute to better overall management of your business.

Tip 1

Invoice your customers as soon as possible. If you are busy, you can easily forget to invoice for goods or services you sold. Also, by invoicing promptly you reduce the time to getting payment for that invoice. Some people I know email invoices to their customers (and post them, too).

Tip 2

Get a receipt or invoice for all expenditure. Suppliers are normally very good at providing invoices (for the opposite reason to that in Tip 1). One-off purchases or smaller expenses like motor fuel are often un-receipted. Make sure you get something on paper for every expense. In doing so, all expenses can be verified by yourself, your accountant and others (like the tax authorities) and can be easily recorded in the day books. You might consider not paying for anything unless an invoice or receipt is provided.

Tip 3

Do your book-keeping regularly, otherwise you might end up with a mountain of work to do. If you don't use some form of accounting soft-ware, you are losing the major advantage of being able to monitor your business performance in a timely fashion. You might also not be able to keep up with deadlines for various payroll tax or VAT returns due.

Tip 4

Do what is called a bank reconciliation on a regular basis – monthly is a good idea. A bank reconciliation means checking your records against the bank statements of the business bank account. By doing this you will: (1) pick up any items paid in/out of the bank account automatically, such as direct debits or electronic payments from customers; and (2) check your day book entries (cash receipts and cheque payments books) against the bank statement and locate errors. The end result should be a matching of your records with the bank's. It is possible that your records might not be exactly the same as the bank's records. For example, you may have written a cheque to a supplier and recorded this in your cheque payments book. The supplier has not yet lodged the cheque in their bank account, so this cheque will not show up on your bank statement as cashed.

Tip 5

Get help if you need it. If you really must concentrate on developing your business and cannot devote any time to book-keeping, get someone to help you. You might have a wife or partner, friend or family member who could help out. Alternatively, some accounting practices offer book-keeping services or there may be a book-keeping 'bureau' in your town. Another option is to automate your book-keeping as much as possible by using some accounting software.

Following these tips will help you have an up-to-date 'set of books', which can provide you with very useful business information, and, of course, keep your accountant and the tax authorities happy.

From the books to the ledgers

You now know how to record business transactions in day books. What happens next? Chapter 5 details how the double-entry system of accounting works. For now, it is enough to know that all transactions from the day books get to what are called 'ledger accounts'. Ledger accounts are recorded in 'ledgers'. There are three ledgers – the sales ledger, the purchases ledger and the nominal (general) ledger. The sales and purchases ledgers hold details of all transactions relating to sales and purchases, grouped by customer and supplier. For example, all transactions related to a customer are grouped – sale invoices, credit notes and cash receipts. Figure 4.9 depicts how the account of John Adams would look (see Figures 4.3 and 4.5 for the day book transactions). Don't worry about the 'two sides' for now; Chapter 5 will give more detail.

FIGURE 4.9

John Adams account

Sales day book	1,150	Sales day book	115
		Cash receipts	2,000

You might find it easier to think of the account of John Adams shown in Figure 4.9 as the customer statement you would send to him. Similarly, each supplier would have an account in the purchases ledger.

The nominal ledger contains 'impersonal' accounts and less detail. Only total amounts from the day books are recorded in the nominal ledger. Figure 4.10 depicts what I term a 'debtors' control' account. This account contains the totals of all customer transactions from the sales day book, cash receipts book and the journal from the earlier examples (see Figures 4.3, 4.5 and 4.8). Look back at the earlier examples and you will see the figures in the account are taken from the total of the sales day book, the total of the 'debtors' column in the cash receipts book and the transaction from the journal.

FIGURE 4.10

Debtors' control account

Sales day book	5,555	Cash receipts book	2,425
		Journal	345

Why three ledgers? The reason dates back to when all book-keeping was manual. One person may have recorded transactions in the day books, a second person transcribed them into the sales or purchases ledger, and, finally, the accountant would take totals from the day books to the nominal ledger. This permitted a segregation of duties, which improves control. Today accounting software can do all this once the source document has been recorded in the software. Several people may still be involved, but the amount of work is a lot less and data is recorded only once.

Day books in Quickbooks software

There are many software packages available which are suitable to small and growing businesses, including Quickbooks, Sage, and TAS Books. I use Quickbooks and recommend it to anyone who has limited accounting knowledge. I find it friendly, easy to use and not full of accounting jargon.

Software like Quickbooks can help any budding entrepreneur with book-keeping and accounting. Any software has one major advantage over a manual system; you only ever need record data once. For example, if you create a sales invoice in accounting software, the invoice goes in the day book, all relevant ledgers and to the financial statements. Other advantages are the ease of reporting and time savings. In this chapter and Chapters 5 and 6, I show you some screenshots from Quickbooks to give you an idea of some of the benefits of accounting software.

The following sections give a brief overview of the recording of transactions in Quickbooks. Some parts skip forward to material from Chapter 5, but you should be able to follow what is going on. The screenshots are from Quickbooks Professional 2008. For space and readability, the shots show only the relevant parts of the screen.

Recording sales and cash receipts from customers in Quickbooks

Quickbooks allows you to record all transactions related to your customers. You can record sales invoices, customer payments and refunds and credits. In the earlier examples this represents the sales day book and cash receipts book. The 'Customer' area of Quickbooks is shown in Figure 4.11.

FIGURE 4.11

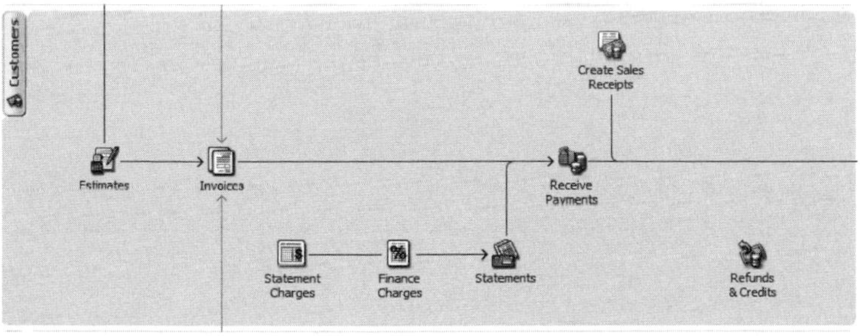

There are icons for 'Invoices' and 'Receive Payments' which represent the sales and cash receipts day books. Let's look at how an invoice is created. Clicking on the 'Invoices' icon displays the screen shown in Figure 4.12.

FIGURE 4.12

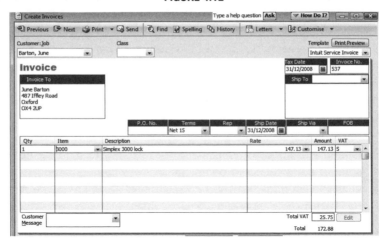

This screen looks very like a manual invoice and does not need a lot of explanation. If this were a handwritten invoice, the information from it would be recorded in the sales day book. This is the equivalent of a sales day book in Quickbooks. Here, all data is input to the screen, the invoice printed and all data stored in the ledgers (see Chapter 5) with a single input.

FIGURE 4.13

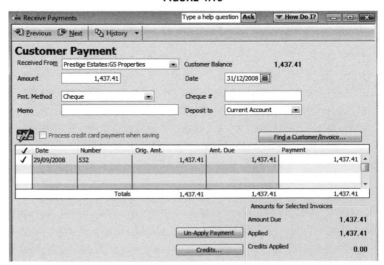

Clicking the 'Receive Payments' icon allows you to enter cash received from customers, as shown in Figure 4.13. The cash received is recorded and also the lodgement to the bank account. This is similar to the earlier example of the cash receipts book. The added benefit here is that the personal ledger account (Prestige Estates) and the nominal ledger accounts (bank, accounts receivable) are also updated (Chapter 5 will give more detail on ledger accounts).

Recording purchases and payments to suppliers in Quickbooks

Quickbooks uses the term 'Bills' instead of invoices when referring to supplier invoices. The 'Suppliers' area of Quickbooks is shown in Figure 4.14.

FIGURE 4.14

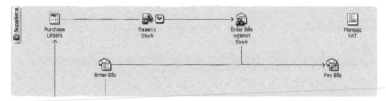

Let's see how bills are recorded and paid. Clicking on the 'Enter Bills' icon displays the screen shown in Figure 4.15. I have recorded a bill from Banbury Locks and Latches. The information input would come from the suppliers' invoice and is equivalent to an entry made in the purchases day book seen earlier. The only difference is that we must specify what kind of expense the invoice relates to. I have identified it as 'Locks and Safes purchases'. This determines the account the transaction goes to in the nominal ledger.

To pay a bill, you click on the 'Pay Bills' icon (see Figure 4.14). You then simply select the bill(s) to be paid – see Figure 4.16 where, for example, I selected City Safe Wholesale. This then records the payment in the cheque payments book, updates the bank account and reduces the amount owed to the supplier.

FIGURE 4.15

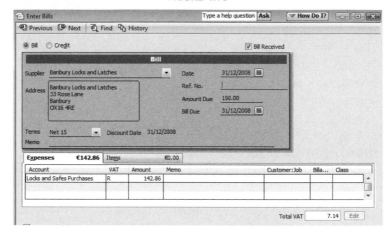

FIGURE 4.16

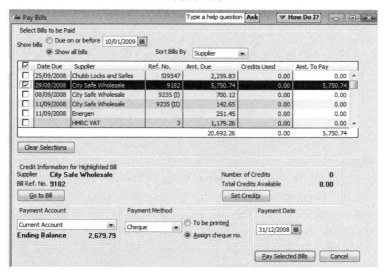

Recording other receipts and payments in Quickbooks

The 'Banking' area of Quickbooks is shown In Figure 4.17. In this area, cheques and receipts from other sources can be recorded.

FIGURE 4.17

Clicking the 'Write Cheques' icon allows you to enter cheque payments which have not been entered using the Pay Bills option. Figure 4.18 shows an example. The screen presents you with what looks like a normal cheque. The details are filled in as if manually completing a cheque. As in the recording of bills, you need to select what kind of expense the cheque is covering – in this example, advertising. It is

FIGURE 4.18

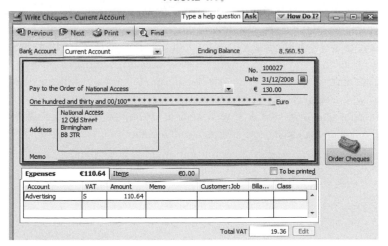

also possible to capture any VAT in this option. Combining this option with the Pay Bills option completes the equivalent of a cheque payments book.

Clicking on the 'Record Deposits' icon shown in Figure 4.17 allows you to enter cash from other sources. I don't show this screen as you simply enter the amount of the deposit and where it came from, for example, bank interest. Combining this option with the 'Receive Payments' option (see Figure 4.13) completes the equivalent of the cash receipts book.

Danger!

If you decide to buy Quickbooks (or other accounting software), check the features before you buy. There are normally four or five versions depending on the size and nature of the business. For example, will you need to trade in more than one currency? Think of the future too – how you think your business will grow, for example. Choosing the right version avoids the need to change or upgrade too soon. You should also check to ensure the software works with the operating system (Windows, Mac or Linux) your computer uses. If in doubt about any software features, seek advice from an accountant.

Danger

From this brief introduction to Quickbooks, I think you will agree that accounting software has a lot to offer. If you are a novice entrepreneur, accounting software can provide quicker ways to record your business transactions, generate understandable reports (some of which I show in later chapters), and provide you with extra time to focus on your business. It can also create professional-looking sales invoices which give your business a good image from the outset.

Key points

→ All source documents of a business are recorded in day books.

→ The day books are the primary source of data for later preparation of financial statements.

→ The layout of day books varies according to the needs of a business.

→ Accounting software makes it easier to capture and record business transactions.

Next step

How are you going to organise yourself so that all source documents of your business are captured and kept in a fashion which allows you to look back easily on any transactions? For example, how are you going to do your sales invoices, where will you file them?

How are you going to record these business transactions? Written, in a spreadsheet or accounting software?

_____

_____

_____

_____

The double-entry system

Chapter Five

Now that you have some knowledge of the day books, it's time to learn about the system which underpins all accounting transactions (no matter how trivial or complex), the double-entry system of accounting. By the end of this chapter you will have an appreciation of the double-entry system and be able at least to understand what accountants are talking about when they start mentioning words like 'debit' and 'credit'.

The chapter starts with a brief history of the origins of double-entry accounting. I then show how the system works and illustrate its workings using examples from the day books in Chapter 4. I give some simple rules to help you understand the system and explain the various types of accounts and how to check that the system has been applied correctly. There will be quite a few new terms. Take your time as this is the key chapter in the book if you want to understand the nuts and bolts of accounting.

The origins of the double-entry system

Business has been transacted for millennia. The first known evidence of recording business transactions dates back to c.8500 BC when merchants in ancient Persia used clay tokens to record how many goods were given to boatmen. Boatmen who delivered the goods downriver were perhaps not always trustworthy, so merchants placed a collection of tokens in a soft clay ball, which dried hard in the sun. The ball (or *bollae*) was handed to the boatman. On arrival at the intended destination the boatman handed the *bollae* over to the buyer, who broke it open and checked the goods.

About 3500 BC, the *bollae* system was replaced with a system of scribing marks on a clay tablet. By about 3000 BC a full number and writing system had evolved. Written accounting records are some of the oldest writings that survive today, dating back to c.3300–3200 BC. These early records were simple notations of wages paid, temple assets, and taxes and tributes to a king or pharaoh.

What we understand today as the double-entry system of accounting was devised by an Italian monk called Luca Pacioli. In 1494 he published a book which detailed the double-entry system still in use today. The next section gives the principles set out by Pacioli over 500 years ago.

Principles of double-entry accounting

The core premise of the double-entry system is that the financial condition and performance of an organisation are recorded in 'accounts'. Each account is a history of money values of a particular aspect of a business. For example, a sales account would record all sales-related transactions and a motor expenses account would record all motor and fuel costs.

The system is called 'double entry' as each transaction must be recorded in at least two accounts. Before I show you how to record transactions, you need to know a little more about a double-entry account.

Layout of a double-entry account

Figure 5.1 shows the layout of a double-entry account. Think of an account as splitting a page into two sides.

FIGURE 5.1

Account header

Debit side	Credit side

The left-hand side of the account is called the debit side, the right-hand the credit side. This is always the case. An account would also have a header, which is just a name to help identify the account – for example, sales account, purchases account, office expenses account.

Time saver

In the account header, you can use the abbreviation a\c for account.

I have already explained that each business transaction is recorded in at least two accounts. In addition, each transaction must have a debit entry and a corresponding credit entry. Accounts are written up in a 'ledger', which traditionally was a specialised hardback book with two sides and various columns for neatness. You can use sheets of A4 paper, an analysis book, or a spreadsheet. However, the term ledger is still used to refer to where the accounts are written or stored.

Which side of an account to use

In Chapter 1, assets, liabilities, capital, revenue and expenditure were mentioned as key terms. By identifying which one of the types of account applies in each transaction, we can introduce some rules for which side of a ledger account to use.

Account type	Debit	Credit
Asset	Increase	Decrease
Liability	Decrease	Increase
Capital	Decrease	Increase
Revenue	Decrease	Increase
Expenditure	Increase	Decrease

To help you remember these rules, the table can be summarised as follows: If an asset is to be increased, you use the debit side of an account, to decrease an asset you use the credit side. The same rule applies to expenditure. Liabilities, capital and revenue use the opposite – increases are on the credit side.

Let's see some examples. Back in Figure 4.2 (on page 53), on 20 October we made a sale to John Adams for £1,150, which was a sale of £1,000 plus £150 VAT. First, ask yourself what accounts are present in this transaction? Write down the three accounts you think are involved here:

1 _____

2 _____

3 _____

The answers: There is an account for sales, an account for John Adams and an account for VAT. Sales (referring to the table above) would be credited as sales increase. John Adams's account will be debited as he represents an asset (he owes us money) and the asset is increasing. Finally, the VAT account is a liability (we owe it to the tax authorities), is being increased (we are collecting it from John Adams), and will be credited. Figure 5.2 shows the three accounts.

FIGURE 5.2

John Adams a\c

20-Oct Sales	1,150	

Sales a\c

	20-Oct John Adams	1,000

VAT a\c

	20-Oct John Adams	150

On each side of each account I have referenced the transaction with the date. I have also included some other reference to link the transaction to the other accounts. You should always try to do this, as it helps anyone trying to follow the transactions in the ledger.

Here's another example. In Figure 4.6 (on page 58), a direct debit payment for telephone was made on 8 October for £120. Again ask yourself what accounts are involved, and write the two accounts below.

1 _____

2 _____

The answer: This time the accounts are telephone and bank. Telephone is an expense, is being increased, and is debited. Bank is an asset, is being decreased, and is credited. Figure 5.3 shows the two accounts. If you refer to the table on page 76, you will be able to put each account entry on the correct side of the accounts each time.

FIGURE 5.3

Telephone a\c

08-Oct Bank	120	

Bank a\c

	08-Oct Telephone	120

Time saver

Some people learn double-entry rules using the phrase 'debit the receiver, credit the giver'. In the first example above, John Adams 'receives', sales 'gives'. In the second, telephone 'receives', bank 'gives'.

Closing off a ledger account

Now you know how to record business transactions in the ledger. As transactions occur, a history of the asset, expense, liability, etc. is built up. At some point, though, you will want to prepare accounts for your business. To do this, you need to 'close off' the ledger accounts. This means that a snapshot of the money value of each ledger account is taken at a point in time, usually a month-end or year-end. The process of closing off is quite simple, all you need do is a little adding and subtracting.

Take a look at Figure 5.4. This shows the ledger account of AB Supplies Ltd. The transactions recorded are those shown earlier in the purchases day book (Figure 4.4, page 55) and the cheque payments book (Figure 4.6, page 58).

FIGURE 5.4

AB Supplies Ltd a\c

03-Oct	Cheque	340	01-Oct	Balance b\d	340
25-Oct	Returns	230	20-Oct	Purchases	700
31-Oct	Balance c\d	470			
		1,040			1,040
			01-Nov	Balance b\d	470

On the credit side of the account you will notice something new – an entry labelled 'balance b\d'. This is the result of a previous closing off of this account. Leaving this aside for a moment, I'll explain how to close off a ledger account. First, add up the transactions on both sides of the account: in Figure 5.4, the debit total is £570, the credit total is £1,040. Next, subtract the smaller total from the larger total: in Figure 5.4 this is £1,040 minus £570, equalling £470. This difference is then entered on the smaller side and called 'balance carried down', which is usually shortened to 'balance c\d'. You can see the balance carried down on the debit side of the account of AB Supplies Ltd. Now, both sides of the account should total to give the same amount, that is, £1,040. A line or two below where you enter the balance carried down, total both sides of the account at the same line level. Last, below the totals you enter a 'balance brought down' (usually shortened to 'balance b\d') on the opposite side. The balance brought down amount is the same amount as the carried down amount.

Ledger accounts are usually closed off when a business wants to prepare a set of accounts. Whatever the date of close, you use this date for the balance carried down, with the balance brought down having the next calendar date.

The process of closing off ledger accounts explains the balance brought down on 1 October in the account AB Supplies Ltd in Figure 5.4. This balance of £340 would have been the balance carried down as at 30 September.

You can present ledger accounts in a three-column format, too. This is much easier if you use a spreadsheet for your ledger accounts. Figure 5.5 shows the account for AB Supplies Ltd in a three-column format. You can see that the balance is calculated after each entry, so you always have a balance carried down available.

FIGURE 5.5

AB Supplies Ltd a\c

	Debit (£)	Credit (£)	Balance (£)
01-Oct Balance b\d		340	340
03-Oct Cheque	340		0
20-Oct Purchases		700	700
25-Oct Returns	230		470

Nominal and personal ledgers

I have already briefly mentioned the different types of ledger (in Chapter 4) – the nominal and personal ledgers. The accounts of AB Supplies Ltd and John Adams above are personal accounts. All personal accounts for customers and suppliers are retained in the personal ledgers. These ledgers are sometimes called 'Accounts receivable' or 'Debtors' ledger for customers, and 'Accounts payable' or 'Creditors' ledger for suppliers. As I said in Chapter 4, transactions recorded in day books are recorded in the ledgers. In the personal ledgers, all transactions – purchases, sales, receipts and payments – are entered to each personal account from the day books. It is therefore possible to track how much each customer owes you and similarly, how much you owe each supplier. Accounts receivable and accounts payable as business functions (departments) are quite often separated in an organisation, one person being responsible for each.

The nominal (or general) ledger is used for all 'non-personal' accounts. This is the ledger traditionally used by accountants, while other accounting staff look after the personal ledgers. Data from the day books is also recorded in the nominal ledger. No personal accounts are held, though. Instead, totals from the day books are entered in what are often referred to as 'control accounts'. Each personal ledger has a control account in the nominal ledger – the accounts receivable (or debtors) control account and the accounts payable (or creditors) control account. In Figure 4.10 (on page 64), I showed a debtors' control account based on the sales day book, cash receipts book and general journal. Figure 5.6 shows the account again, properly closed off, of course. A similar creditors' (or accounts payable) control account could be prepared from the purchases day book, cheque payments and general journal.

FIGURE 5.6

Debtors control account

Sales day book	5,555	Cash receipts book	2,425
		Journal – bad debt	345
		Balance c\d	2,785
	5,555		5,555
Balance b\d	2,785		

The debit side amount of £5,555 is the total of the sales day book from Figure 4.3 (see page 54). In the personal ledger this figure would be broken down into the various personal accounts. The corresponding credit entry for this is to the sales account in the nominal ledger. Similarly, the credit side amount of £2,425 is the total cash received from customers in the cash receipts book (see Figure 4.5 on page 56). The corresponding debit entry for this is to the bank account in the nominal ledger. Finally, the credit side amount of £345 originated in the general journal (see Figure 4.8 on page 60). The corresponding debit entry for this is to a bad debts account in the nominal ledger.

In other words

In the ledgers, the **personal ledgers** hold details of all individual transactions for customer and suppliers. The **nominal ledger** holds all other accounts, which includes a summary 'control account' for each of the personal ledgers.

The trial balance

If the rules of double-entry accounting are applied correctly, the total of debits should equal the total credits. As ledger entries form the basis for financial statements (see Chapter 6), they need to be correct. To check if the ledger accounts have applied the rules of double entry, something called a trial balance is prepared.

A trial balance is prepared by taking all account balances (i.e. the balances b\d) and listing them in two columns according to whether or not they are debit or credit balances. Figure 5.7 shows an example.

First, I have taken all data in this example from the day books in Chapter 4, by completing the ledger accounts and calculating the balances. As an exercise, do this yourself to see if you get the same answer.

FIGURE 5.7

Debtors control account

Sales	5,555	Cash receipts	2,425
		Journal – bad debt	345
		Balance c\d	2,785
	5,555		5,555
Balance b\d	2,785		

Creditors control account

Bank	340	Purchases	2,375
Balance c\d	2,035		
	2,375		2,375
		Balance b\d	2,035

Bank account

Debtors	2,425	Cheques	6,400
Utilities refund	10		
Cash sales	240		
Balance c\d	3,725		
	6,400		6,400
		Balance b\d	3,725

Bad debts account

Debtors	345	Balance c\d	345
Balance b\d	345		

Sales account

Balance c\d	4,740	Debtors	4,540
		Cash sales	200
	4,740		4,740
		Balance b\d	4,740

Purchases account

Creditors	1,940	Balance c\d	1,940
Balance b\d	1,940		

FIGURE 5.7

VAT account

Creditors	435	Debtors	1,015
Bank	300	Cash sales	40
Balance c\d	320		
	1,055		1,055
		Balance b/d	320

Utilities account

Bank	130	Cash receipts	10
		Balance c\d	120
	130		130
Balance b\d	120		

Wages account

Bank	500	Balance c\d	500
Balance b\d	500		

Telephone account

Bank	120	Balance c\d	120
Balance b\d	120		

Vans account

Bank	5,000	Balance c\d	5,000
Balance b\d	5,000		

Petty cash account

Bank	10	Balance c\d	10
Balance b\d	10		

FIGURE 5.7

Trial balance of Trilby Traders as at 31 October

	Debit (£)	Credit (£)
Debtors	2,785	
Creditors		2,035
Bank		3,725
Bad debts	345	
Sales		4,740
Purchases	1,940	
VAT		320
Utilities	120	
Wages	500	
Telephone	120	
Vans	5,000	
Petty cash	10	
	10,820	10,820

I have taken the balances brought down (balance b\d) from each ledger account and simply placed them in the respective column of the trial balance. For example, the debtors' balance b\d is £2,785 debit, so this goes in the debit column. The debit and credit totals in the trial balance are equal, proving I have correctly applied the principles of the double-entry system outlined above.

Danger!

If a trial balance does not balance, don't leave it. You should go back through the ledger and resolve any mistakes.

If a trial balance does balance, does this mean that all figures and ledger accounts are 100 per cent accurate? The answer is no, for a number of reasons:

→ Transactions may have been completely omitted from the day books and thus never get recorded in the ledgers. For example, a supplier's invoice may have been misplaced and not entered anywhere. This type of error is referred to as an error of omission.

→ A correct entry may have been made to an incorrect account. For example, a sale to a customer, A. Baker, was posted to the debit side of the ledger account for A. Barker. The debits and credits will be equal, but incorrect. This type of error is referred to as an error of commission.

→ An entry could be completely reversed. For example, you post a credit sale to the credit side of a debtors' account and the debit side of the sales account.

→ Two errors might compensate each other. For example, you may have over added both the purchases and sales account by £100. As the purchases would normally have a debit balance, and sales a credit balance, one error cancels the other.

→ An entry could have been incorrectly taken from the day books. For example, the total sales in the sales day book might read £18,000, but you misread this as £13,000 and entered it in the sales and debtors' accounts as £13,000. This type of error is referred to as an error of original entry

→ Finally, an entry could be made to the wrong class of account. For example, the purchase of a delivery van could be debited to a motor expenses account (expense) and not to a motor vans account (asset). This type of error is called an error of principle.

Locating errors

If the trial balance does not balance, you have made a mistake somewhere in your ledger entries or trial balance preparation. How to find the mistake is the problem. There are a number of things you can do:

→ Recheck the totals of each column of the trial balance to make sure your addition is correct.

→ Make sure the balances from each ledger account are in the correct column of the trial balance.

→ Make sure you have transcribed all balances correctly from the ledger accounts to the trial balance.

→ If the difference on the trial balance is divisible evenly by nine, you have transposed figures somewhere. For example, you have used £910 in one place and £901 in another. This can help find differences a little quicker.

If these steps do not help, you will have to check each ledger account to ensure your adding/subtracting is correct.

The trial balance and financial statements

A trial balance also has another important function and that is to help in the preparation of financial statements (the income statement and balance sheet). If you look at the trial balance in Figure 5.7, you can see it is at a month end. Although a trial balance can be prepared at any time, it is more often prepared at a month or year end to help prepare the financial statements. It is very useful for this purpose as it is a summary of all accounts from which we can pick (1) the income and expenses for the income statement, and (2) assets, liabilities and capital for the balance sheet. Chapter 6 gives more detail on this.

Ledger accounts and the trial balance in Quickbooks

In Chapter 4 I explained how accounting software like Quickbooks does a lot of the work once a business transaction (invoice, cheque, cash receipt, etc.) is entered. Let's look at how Quickbooks prepares ledger accounts. Take, for example, the payment made to City Safe Wholesale for £5,750.74 shown on page 68. This payment would be debited to the accounts payable control account (and, of course, the personal account for City Safe Wholesale) and credited to the bank account. The screenshots in Figures 5.8 and 5.9 show the ledger

FIGURE 5.8

Type	Date	Num	Name	Memo	Split	Amount	Balance
Current Account							**8,880.78**
Cheque	10/12/2008	SO	Thames Council		-SPLIT-	-111.00	8,769.78
Cheque	15/12/2008	DD	National Bank	quarterly loan r...	-SPLIT-	-209.25	8,560.53
Cheque	31/12/2008	100027	National Access		-SPLIT-	-130.00	8,430.53
Bill Pmt -Cheque	31/12/2008	12345	Cty Safe Wholesale		Accounts Payable	-5,750.74	2,679.79
Payment	31/12/2008		Prestige Estates GS Pr...		Accounts Recei...	1,437.41	4,117.20
Total Current Account						-4,763.58	4,117.20

FIGURE 5.9

Type	Date	Num	Name	Memo	Split	Amount	Balance
Accounts Payable							**-20,158.58**
Bill	01/12/2008		Stuart Leven		-SPLIT-	-1,000.00	-21,158.58
Bill Pmt -Cheque	31/12/2008	12345	City Safe Wholesale		Current Account	5,750.74	-15,407.84
Total Accounts Payable						4,750.74	-15,407.84

entries made in the general ledger by Quickbooks at the time of making the payment (i.e. entering it in the cheque payments book).

The screenshot in Figure 5.8 shows the payment (circled) in the bank account (called Current account in the example). This looks a little different from the manually drafted accounts I have shown earlier: it is more like the three-column format. Depending on which accounting software package you use, what you see may be different. Quickbooks does not use the terms debit and credit very often, its aim being to keep things simple for non-accountants. In this example, the payment is shown with a minus sign, which Quickbooks adopts for credits. Now look at the accounts payable account in Figure 5.9. The payment is again circled. This time, the payment is a positive number, which Quickbooks adopts for debits.

Looking at both, you can see a number of useful things. After each entry, the balance column is recalculated, which is the balance brought forward. Also, the column 'Split' gives a reference to the other general ledger account in the transaction. Finally, something which I cannot show in a textbook is also possible. With a simple double click on the payment to City Safe Wholesale, Quickbooks will display the original payment (day book) entry made, and in turn lead to the original bill (source document). This 'drill down' facility is available in most accounting software and is extremely useful for quickly getting a break-down of any figure.

Trial balance

In the ledger accounts from Quickbooks shown above, the balance on the account is constantly recalculated after each transaction. Closing off accounts is therefore not needed. This means you can run a trial balance at any time. Figure 5.10 shows a trial balance from the Quickbooks sample company.

It looks just like a trial balance prepared manually. There are a lot of accounts listed in this example. You might have noticed there is logic to the order of the accounts. First, asset accounts; then liabilities; capital; income (sales); and expenses. This is not a rule, more a convention within the accounting world.

FIGURE 5.10

	Debit	Credit
Current Account	▶ 8,880.78 ◀	
Cash Account	49.55	
Accounts Receivable	14,989.82	
Stock	1,287.44	
Undeposited Funds	4,118.68	
Plant & Equipment:Cost Plant & Equip	850.00	
Computer equipment:Cost Computer Equip	800.00	
Vehicles:Cost Vehicles	3,750.00	
Accounts Payable		20,158.58
Credit Card Account		1,994.96
Bank Loan		2,700.00
Director's Loan		3,500.00
Payroll Liabilities		349.67
VAT Liability		528.67
Share Capital		1,000.00
Retained Earnings		795.00
Sales		35,930.04
Locks and Safes Purchases	19,334.48	
Advertising	500.00	
Bank Service Charges	11.70	
Dues and Subscriptions	12.60	
Insurance	227.83	
Interest Expense	118.50	
Motor Expense	138.77	
Office Supplies	251.47	
Payroll Expenses	5,996.84	
Rent & Rates	6,555.00	
Software Expense	34.03	
Telephone	246.97	
Utilities	214.00	
Interest Received		16.44
Subletting Income		1,695.00
Dividends	500.00	
TOTAL	68,668.36	68,668.36

Finally, all accounting software has a saving grace in that it is impossible for the trial balance not to balance. This is simply because as transactions are entered, the debit and credit elements must be in balance. Otherwise, the software will not permit the transaction to be recorded.

Key points

→ The double-entry system of accounting is used to record all business transactions.

→ Transactions are recorded in 'ledgers'.

→ Each business transaction is recorded with two ledger entries, one debit, and one credit.

→ The total of all debits will equal the total of all credits. The trial balance proves this.

→ A trial balance is useful in the preparation of the financial statements.

Next step

Before proceeding to Chapter 6, be sure you understand clearly the content of all the chapters so far. If you plan to use software, make a note of what software might be most useful for *your* business. Go ahead and purchase it and as you read through the rest of this book begin to enter the relevant figures for your business.

_____

_____

_____

_____

An introduction to financial statements

We're now ready to see how two basic financial statements, the income statement and balance sheet, are prepared. The income statement is also known as the profit and loss account. The latter term is more commonly used for small business. The term 'income statement' is required to be used by European Union law (since 2004) for public companies, and many private companies also use it. I adopt it in this book as it is increasingly more commonly used in the business world.

There are two purposes of this chapter: (1) to use the trial balance to prepare financial statements, and (2) to introduce some adjustments/ additions which are normally required to the trial balance before 'final' financial statements are available. To keep things simple, this chapter provides examples assuming the business is a sole trader. The next chapter will deal with financial statements of limited companies.

The worst crime against working people is a company which fails to operate at a profit.

SAMUEL GOMPERS (first president of the American Federation of Labor)

The income statement

As an entrepreneur, your business objective may not always be to maximise profits. Having said that, if a business does not make a profit it will not survive. How do you know if you have made a profit or not? Preparing an income statement will tell you.

An income statement is the financial statement which shows the income and expenses of a business and, therefore, its profit or loss. In other words, it depicts the financial performance of a business. If you are a sole trader, the income statement does not have to conform to any particular layout. However, accounting standards (rules followed by accountants), which dictate the layout of financial statements for companies, are often followed by accountants for other business forms.

The trial balance of Trilby Traders from Chapter 5 is shown again below in Figure 6.1. I use this to prepare a basic income statement. This means we use the trial balance to identify the income and expenses of the business.

FIGURE 6.1

Trial balance of Trilby Traders as at 31 October

	Debit (£)	Credit (£)
Debtors	2,785	
Creditors		2,035
Bank		3,725
Bad debts	345	
Sales		4,740
Purchases	1,940	
VAT		320
Utilities	120	
Wages	500	
Telephone	120	
Vans	5,000	
Petty cash	10	
	10,820	10,820

Remember, the debit column of the trial balance contains assets and expense account balances, the credit column contains income, liabilities and capital. Looking at each item on the trial balance, the only income account is sales. The expenses are bad debts, purchases, utilities, wages and telephone. This is all we need to prepare the income statement. Before we do, take a look at the sample income statement for company XYZ on the next page.

Danger!

The word income in an income statement means income from operations, that is, income generated from what your business does. This normally means sales income. Other income, such as bank interest, will be indentified separately in an income statement.

Danger

Income statement of XYZ for the year ended 31/12/200X

	£	£
Sales		10,000
Cost of sales		(4,000)
Gross profit		6,000
Light and heat	500	
Motor expenses	1000	
Insurance	600	
Wages	400	
		2,500
Operating profit		3,500

A few items need some explanation. **Cost of sales** is a figure closely related to the sales figure. The cost of a sale may be identified as a product is made. For example, in a custom engineering business, costs may be accumulated for each order. More often, cost of sales is calculated only when an income statement is required. For now, think of cost of sales as the purchase price of goods you sell. Additional costs, like transport or customs duties, are also included in cost of sales.

Gross profit is sales less cost of sales. This is simply the profit from trading, before deducting any running costs/expenses. Gross profit less expenses is the operating (net) profit. **Operating profit** is the amount of money generated by the normal trading activities of a business. As mentioned earlier, a business may have other sources of income, such as bank interest, which would now be added to this figure.

Back to Trilby Traders: taking the income and expenses from the trial balance in Figure 6.1, the income statement for the month of October would look like that shown in Figure 6.2.

You might notice that the heading of the income statement says for 'the month ended 31 October'. This makes sense, as to compare incomes and expenses over a time period means you can calculate a profit or loss for that time period. This will change for the balance sheet.

The headings of financial statements take the form 'who', 'what' and 'when', that is, who is the business? what financial statement is it? when is it for? That's it. Income statements (no matter how complex the business) list income, expenditure and profits/losses. Now let's see what making a profit means for your business.

FIGURE 6.2

Income statement of Trilby Traders for the month
ended 31 October 2008

	(£)	(£)
Sales		4,740
Cost of Sales		(1,940)
Gross Profit		2,800
Bad debts	345	
Utilities	120	
Wages	500	
Telephone	120	
		1,085
Operating profit		1,715

The effect of profit on capital

Above, Trilby Traders made a profit of £1,715. What does this mean for
the business owner? It means the value of the capital of the business
has increased by £1,715. Of course, if you make a profit chances are
you will have to pay tax, but let's ignore that for a moment and assume
no tax is due. Do you recall the accounting equation from Chapter 1? It
stated assets minus liabilities equals capital. Take a look at Figure 6.3
which shows a simple list of assets and liabilities.

FIGURE 6.3

Tom's business

	£
Assets	
Cash	17,000
Van	5,000
Inventories (stock)	3,000
	25,000
Liabilities	
Bank loan	12,000
Trade payables	3,000
	15,000
Capital (balance)	10,000

As you can see, the accounting equation shows the capital as £10,000. Tom's business has inventories (stock) valued which cost £3,000. Suppose he sells the inventory for £5,000, thus making a profit of £2,000. This also means his inventory is now nil and, assuming the monies from the sale are lodged to the bank account, the cash balance is £22,000 (£17,000 plus £5,000). These changes to the assets and liabilities are shown in Figure 6.4.

FIGURE 6.4

Tom's business

	£
Assets	
Cash	22,000
Van	5,000
Inventories (stock)	–
	27,000
Liabilities	
Bank loan	12,000
Trade payables	3,000
	15,000
Capital (balance)	12,000

As the accounting equation must hold, the capital figure is now £12,000. This is the original capital (£10,000) plus the profit on the sale (£2,000). From this example you can see that profit increases capital. Likewise, a loss will decrease capital.

As a sole trader you might want to withdraw some of the profits made, to cover your own personal living expenses. Any such amounts are called drawings. Drawings are not the same as wages, since wages relate to employees and you can't employ yourself. Drawings are in fact a reduction in the capital of the business. Most sole traders take some form of cash drawing on a regular basis – after all, you have to live and eat.

Additionally, you are likely to have to pay tax on profits. This is also a reduction in the capital of the business.

Returning to Trilby Traders, let's assume the tax on profits for the month of October is £215 and now, knowing a profit has been made, the owner decides to take drawings of £500. This leaves profit of £1,000 in the business, and the capital will increase by this amount. The movements on capital are shown not in the income statement, but a balance sheet, which I'll explain below. From what I have shown of the effect of profit on capital, you might have guessed by now that the profits/losses from the income statement are a link between it and the balance sheet.

The balance sheet

A balance sheet is simply a list of the assets, liabilities and capital of a business at any point in time. It is often referred to as a statement of the financial position of a business, as it shows what the business has (assets), what it owes (liabilities) and how it is financed (capital), at a particular date. You already know what assets, liabilities and capital are from Chapter 1, so let's see how they appear in the balance sheet. The name 'balance sheet' also suggests something must balance. The elements of the balance sheet are the same as the components of the accounting equation, so by definition the balance sheet will balance. Or look at it another way:

1 we start off with a trial balance that balances;
2 we take all income and expenses in the trial balance to the income statement and work out a profit or loss;

3 we take the profit to the balance sheet with all remaining items from the trial balance;

4 thus, the balance sheet would have to balance.

Before I show you a balance sheet, let me explain how assets and liabilities are grouped for the purposes of the balance sheet.

Classification of assets and liabilities in a balance sheet

For the purposes of clarity and understanding, assets and liabilities are not listed haphazardly in a balance sheet. Normally assets and liabilities are classified in a number of groupings, which I mentioned briefly in Chapter 1. Let's look at them in detail.

Current assets

These are assets which are short-term in nature. Current assets normally meet one of the following characteristics:

→ they are held for use or resale by the business as part of normal day-to-day operations;

→ they are expected to be sold within one year;

→ they are held primarily for trading purposes;

→ they are cash, or equivalent to cash (i.e. can be sold for cash quickly).

The most common current assets are inventories (stocks), amounts owed by customers (trade receivables/debtors) and cash/cash in the bank. The level of each held by a business depends on the nature of the business. For example, a service business is not likely to have any inventories.

Non-current assets

Non-current (or fixed) assets are assets which are not current assets. They are held by a business for the long term and often have a product-ive use. Examples would be premises, vans, and office furniture. What is classified as a non-current asset depends on the nature of the business. For example, a car may be a non-current asset of your business, but would be a current asset (i.e. inventory) of a car manufacturer.

Current liabilities

Current liabilities are amounts owed which will be paid within one year. To be a little more precise, they normally meet one of the following criteria:

→ they are paid within the normal course of business;
→ they are due to be paid within one year of the balance sheet date;
→ they are held for trading purposes,
→ there is no right to extend the settlement period beyond one year.

Examples of current liabilities are amounts owing to suppliers (trade payables), amounts owing to tax authorities and a bank overdraft.

Non-current liabilities

Non current liabilities are liabilities other than current liabilities. Typical examples are long-term bank loans. Quite often, a balance sheet will show bank loans split into the portion due within one year, which is shown as a current liability, and the portion due after one year, shown as a non-current liability.

Layout of the balance sheet

A balance sheet is normally presented in a vertical layout, as shown in Figure 6.5. This layout shows assets grouped on the top portion of the balance sheet, and capital and liabilities on the bottom portion.

As you can see, the total of the assets is equal to the total of liabilities plus capital, so the balance sheet balances. You may see a balance sheet presented in a variety of different ways, but it will always have two totals which equal each other. For example, I could show assets and deduct liabilities on the upper portion, with just capital in the lower portion.

FIGURE 6.5

Balance sheet of XYZ as at 31/12/2008

	£000	£000
Non-current assets		
Property		45
Plant and equipment		30
Motor van		19
		94
Current assets		
Inventories	23	
Trade receivables	18	
Cash at bank	12	
		53
		147
Capital		
Owners capital		60
Non-current liabilities		
Long term bank loan		50
Current liabilities		
Trade payables	30	
Taxation owing	7	37
		147

Let's return to Trilby Traders. From the trial balance and income statement earlier, the balance sheet is as set out in Figure 6.6.

Most figures are taken straight from the trial balance. In this example, the owner's capital is simply the profit from the income statement. This will not always be the case. Normally, the capital figure shown on the balance sheet is a single figure. It may consist of capital introduced to the business, profits made, drawings, and taxation paid. A capital account often forms part of the accounts of a sole trader. This is simply a more detailed analysis of the movements of owners' capital. Figure 6.7 shows an example.

FIGURE 6.6

Balance sheet of Trilby Traders as at 31/10/2008

	£	£
Non-current assets		
Motor van		5,000
		5,000
Current assets		
Debtors	2,785	
Petty cash	10	
		2,795
		7,795
Capital		
Owners capital		1,715
Current liabilities		
Creditors	2,035	
VAT owing	320	
Bank overdraft	3,725	6,080
		7,795

FIGURE 6.7

Capital Account of XYZ for the year ended 31/12/2008

	£
Capital introduced	50,000
Profit for year	45,000
Drawings	(30,000)
Income tax	(10,000)
Capital as at 31/12/2008	55,000

Here you can see how the capital was added to (profits and capital introduced) and reduced (drawings by the owner). The capital balance of £55,000 will be the opening capital for the next year, to which profits are added, drawings subtracted, etc.

That's it for the balance sheet. Now that you know the basics of both the income statement and balance sheet, let's see some more items that need to be examined when these statements are being prepared.

Preparing the financial statements

To prepare an income statement and balance sheet directly from the trial balance is not fully correct. Even if you are pretty good at keeping your day books and ledgers (either manually or using software), there will be some additional work needed to prepare financial statements. Typically, the process would be something like this:

1 Get a trial balance to ensure it balances.

2 Check the trial balance for any odd looking figures (maybe a balance looks too large). If so, check to see if errors were made in the day books or ledgers. Correct any errors and get a new trial balance.

3 Provide for/adjust expenses so that all expenses relate only to the period of the income statement.

4 Do an inventory count and put a value on it.

5 Calculate depreciation on non-current assets.

6 Prepare the income statement and balance sheet.

Businesses that keep manual records often leave all these steps to their accountant. If you use software, steps 4 and 5 may happen automatically. Accountants often refer to the above steps as 'year-end adjustments'. I'll now explain these in more detail.

Accruals and prepayments

The accruals concept was introduced in Chapter 1. To refresh your memory, it means that income and expenditure is accounted for when a transaction occurs, not when cash is paid. It is often called the 'matching' concept, too, as it means revenues and costs should be matched against each other when a transaction occurs.

In practical terms this means that when financial statement are prepared, bills for expenses within the accounting period only (i.e. the period of the income statement) need to be included. It is highly unlikely that all bills will have been received when the income statement is being prepared, and thus need to be 'accrued' for. Likewise, some expenses may have been paid during an accounting period, but relate to a later period. Such 'prepayments' need to be removed.

Consider the following example. Fred's accounting year ends on 30 June. He is preparing his income statement. He discovers he has not yet received a mobile phone bill for June. His normal monthly bill is £80. He is also missing a bill for electricity for the month of June, which he estimates would be £50. Fred rents his office for £10,000 per annum and pays this up front on 1 January each year.

What are the accruals and prepayment in this example? Jot your answer below.

_____

_____

_____

_____

The mobile phone bill and the electricity bill need to be accrued for as they are costs within Fred's accounting year and should be matched against his income for the same period in the income statement. It does not matter if his estimates are not 100 per cent accurate. Half of the rent (January to June) relates to Fred's income statement for this year, half to next year. Items like these are of course recorded in the day books – the general journal. In fact Figure 6.8 shows the general journal entries in Fred's books

FIGURE 6.8

Fred's Business
General journal

	DR (£)	CR (£)
Telephone	80	
Accrued expenses		80
(Telephone bill for June accrued)		
Light and heat	50	
Accrued expenses		50
(Telephone bill for June accrued)		
Rent		5,000
Prepaid expenses	5,000	
(Rent paid in advance on 1 Jan)		

You can see the telephone and light and heat accounts are being debited, or increased. This is what you would expect as the bills not yet received would increase the expense for the year. An account called 'accrued expenses' is being credited in both cases. This is, as you might expect, a liability, or more correctly a current liability, in the balance sheet. The rent account is being credited, reducing the expense as the prepaid portion of the rent does not relate to this year. The corresponding debit is to an account called 'prepaid expenses', which is treated as a current asset in the balance sheet.

As shown above, accruals and prepayments affect both the income statement and the balance sheet. Accruals in particular may be estimates of expenses for which bills have not yet been received. For this reason, accountants and tax inspectors keep a close eye on accruals in particular, as it is easy to 'stick in an accrual' to reduce profits! This aside, accruals and prepayments need to be addressed when preparing the income statement and balance sheet as not to do so will give an inaccurate picture of the true profit of the business for an accounting period.

Inventory valuation

If your business buys and sells goods, it is likely you will have inventories at the end of an accounting year. The inventory was purchased during the year, with invoices recorded as a purchase in the purchases day book (or in your accounting software).

Is inventory held at the end of a year a cost for the current account year or the next? Write what you think below.

_____

_____

_____

_____

This is another case of the accruals concept in action, as the cost of the goods will not be expensed (or matched) against a sale until the following year at least.

So how do you value your inventory? First you need to do what is called an inventory count or stock-take. This means counting the inventories your business has. The effort required to do this depends on your business. Some tips on doing a good inventory count are given below.

Time saver

Here are some tips to help you conduct a good inventory count:

→ Pick a time when your business is very quiet, preferably closed.

→ Count all items, regardless of location, age or condition.

→ Take a note of any items damaged.

→ If several people are involved, create a summary of all items.

→ Put a value on all items.

Many businesses use inventory control software. Even Quickbooks has a simple inventory control module. With such software programs, you may be able to get an inventory report and use this as a basis for the count (i.e. checking that what the reports says should be in stock is in stock).

Accounting has a rule that inventories should be valued at the lower of cost or net realisable value. **Cost** means the amount for which the items were bought, including delivery charges, customs duties, etc. (but not VAT). **Net realisable value** means the sales value less any costs required to make the item saleable. This usually only applies to items which are damaged. For example, a furniture store might have a table which got scratched. It had cost £500, but can now be sold only for £450. Thus, its value is £450.

Once a value has been placed on inventory, it is used to reduce the cost of sales figure in the income statement. Therefore, cost of sales in an income statement comprises:

Opening inventory + Purchases − Closing inventory

Inventory is also an asset, more correctly a current asset. The value of inventory at the end of the accounting period is thus entered in the balance sheet under current assets. Again, the value of inventory would be entered in the general journal and might look something like that set out for Fred's business in Figure 6.9.

FIGURE 6.9

Fred's business
General journal

	DR (£)	CR (£)
Inventory – current asset	1,564	
Costs of sales		1,564
(Year end inventory value)		

The value of inventory is important since it affects gross profit. A higher closing inventory value will lower the cost of sales. A lower cost of sales, in turn, means a higher gross profit. Not bad, you might think, but higher profits means higher taxes. Or, if you were cynical, you might think a business could build up inventory to deliberately inflate profits! Let's just say that if your business had a manager who was paid a bonus on profits, increasing inventory might increase the bonus.

In addition to getting an inventory value for accounting purposes, there are other reasons for performing a check on your inventories. The most obvious reason is to prevent pilferage. An acquaintance of mine is the accountant for a chain of very busy high-street newsagents. The store manager is required to count some items (cigarettes, lottery scratch cards and travel tickets, for example) daily.

Finally, as inventory is an asset of your business, you should manage it as such. This means keeping inventories secure, organised, at the correct temperatures, and so on, to ensure good condition is maintained at all times.

Depreciation

Non-current (fixed) assets are used by a business to help it generate revenue and make profits. In Chapter 1, capital expenditure on assets was distinguished from normal day-to-day expenditure. Expenditure on non-current assets contributes to the revenue generated by the business, but over a period of time. A delivery van may be good for five years and you might think it reasonable to spread its cost over five years. This does actually happen and in accounting it is called depreciation.

In other words

Depreciation is an accounting technique used to spread the cost of non-current assets over a number of years.

Depreciation apportions part of the cost of a non-current asset that has been used up in an accounting period. It is an estimating technique and will not be 100 per cent accurate. The two most common methods of estimating depreciation are known as the straight line method and the reducing-balance method. Figure 6.10 shows how the straight-line method works

FIGURE 6.10

Straight-line depreciation method

Cost of asset (£)	10,000
Residual value (£)	2,000
Estimated life	4 years
Depreciation per annum	

$$\frac{\text{Cost} - \text{residual value}}{\text{Useful life}} = \frac{8,000}{4}$$

Annual depreciation (£)	2,000

As the name suggests, the straight-line method assumes an asset provides benefits evenly over its useful life. In the example in Figure 6.10, the residual (scrap) value is deducted from the cost as this amount reflects what the asset might be sold for after four years and this reduces the cost.

Figure 6.11 shows the reducing-balance method. With this method, the depreciation charge is based on the reduced balance (cost minus

An introduction to financial statements

depreciation to date). This means a higher depreciation charge occurs in earlier years.

FIGURE 6.11

Reducing-balance depreciation method

	£
Cost of asset	10,000
Depreciation to be 20% of reduced balance	
Year 1 depreciation	2,000
Year 1 reduced balance	8,000
Year 2 depreciation	
(20% of £8,000)	1,600
Year 2 reduced balance	6,400
Year 3 depreciation	
(20% of £6,400)	1,280
Year 3 reduced balance	5,120
(and so on...)	

Which depreciation method do you use? If the asset provides equal benefits, or the wear and tear is equal each year, then the straight-line method might be best. For example, buildings and office furniture are often depreciated using this method. When assets become less efficient over time, the reducing-balance method is often used. Motor vehicles and machinery are often depreciated using this method.

The depreciation charge for each year is an expense in the income statement. It is also shown in the balance sheet as accumulated depreciation, which is the sum of depreciation charges for all years. For example, using Figure 6.11, the income statement for Year 2 would show the depreciation expense as £1,600. The balance sheet for the same year would show the asset at £6,400 under the fixed-asset heading.

To summarise, an initial trial balance is the starting point in preparing the income statement and balance sheet. Expenses are examined to see if accruals or prepayments apply, inventory is counted and valued, and depreciation on non-current assets is calculated. If you can do all this, you will have quite accurate financial statements. If you can't, it does not mean that your financial statements are not good enough to help you make business decisions. Totally accurate information is not normally required for routine business decisions.

Financial statements in Quickbooks

As I said in Chapter 5, Quickbooks automatically compiles financial statements for you as business transactions are entered. Let's look at some of the financial statement reports Quickbooks can generate.

Figure 6.12 is an example of an income statement (profit and loss account). The layout, while containing more expenses than the earlier examples, is pretty much the same. Only one year is shown in this example. You can select any time period (year, month, quarter, or custom dates) and also place comparatives.

Likewise, a balance sheet can be printed as shown in Figure 6.13. This shows the assets and liabilities in the upper portion, with capital in the lower portion. Again, this report can be printed for any time period, with comparatives.

In addition to standard reports like those above, most accounting software provides some form of graphical representation. These give a useful snapshot of the business in a very user-friendly manner. For example, Quickbooks provides an income and expense graph by month (see Figure 6.14). It provides a quick way to see if your business is making a profit or a loss, and a breakdown of expenses by type. Many people I know who are not accounting literate use this method each month to see how their business is doing.

Web bonus

At our website, **www.forentrepreneursbooks.com**, click on the 'Book-keeping and Accounting for Entrepreneurs' button. Click on the link for Chapter 6, where you will find some templates in spreadsheet form which you may find useful in setting up the underlying accounts needed to create an income statement and balance sheet.

FIGURE 6.12

Sample Ltd
Profit & Loss
January through December 2007

	Jan – Dec 2007
Ordinary Income/Expense	
Income	
Sales	36,890.96
Services	244,174.44
Total Income	281,065.40
Cost of Goods Sold	
Materials	98,478.87
Other Supplies	1,834.95
Sundry Hand Tools	906.28
Total COGS	101,220.10
Gross Profit	179,845.30
Expense	
Advertising	1,128.00
Bank charges	393.63
Cash Discounts	1,937.32
Insurance	1,722.77
Motor Expense	10,967.04
Office Supplies	714.13
Payroll Expenses	54,785.36
Postage and Delivery	109.00
Professional Fees	
Accounting	660.00
Professional Fees – Other	330.00
Total Professional Fees	990.00
Rent	1,191.63
Safety Expenses	687.36
Telephone	1,994.51
Travel & Ent	
Travel	577.74
Total Travel & Ent	577.74
Waste Disposal	779.73
Total Expense	77,978.22
Net Ordinary Income	101,867.08
Net Income	**101,867.08**

Book-keeping and Accounts for Entrepreneurs

FIGURE 6.13

Sample Ltd
Balance Sheet
As at 31 March 2008

	31 Mar 08
ASSETS	
Current Assets	
Other Current Assets	
Stock	911.78
Total Other Current Assets	911.78
Accounts Receivable	
Accounts Receivable	254.47
Total Accounts Receivable	254.47
Cash at bank and in hand	
Current Account	8,498.47
Cash Account	101.29
Total Cash at bank and in hand	8,599.76
Total Current Assets	9,766.01
Current Liabilities	
Accounts Payable	
Accounts Payable	971.01
Total Accounts Payable	971.01
Other Current Liabilities	
Bank Loan	3,000.00
Director's Loan	4,000.00
Total Other Current Liabilities	7,000.00
Total Current Liabilities	7,971.01
NET CURRENT ASSETS	1,795.00
TOTAL ASSETS LESS CURRENT LIABILITIES	1,795.00
NET ASSETS	**1,795.00**
Capital and Reserves	
Share Capital	1,000.00
Profit for the Year	795.00
Shareholder funds	**1,795.00**

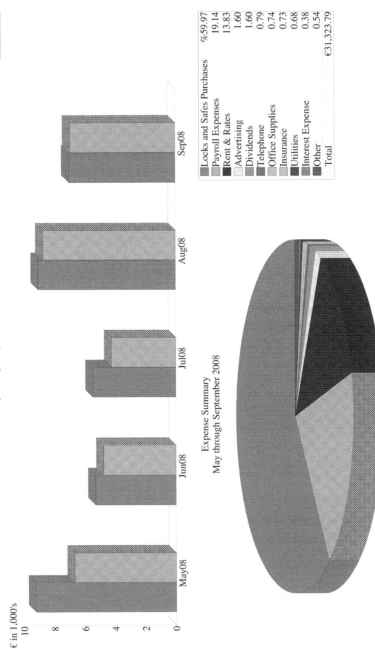

FIGURE 6.14

Income and Expense by Month
May through September 2008

€ in 1,000's

| Income |
| Expense |

Expense Summary
May through September 2008

Locks and Safes Purchases	%	59.97
Payroll Expenses		19.14
Rent & Rates		13.83
Advertising		1.60
Dividends		1.60
Telephone		0.79
Office Supplies		0.74
Insurance		0.73
Utilities		0.68
Interest Expense		0.38
Other		0.54
Total		€31,323.79

By Account

Key points

→ The income statement and balance sheet are two key financial statements of a business.

→ The income statement shows the financial performance (profit or loss) of a business.

→ The balance sheet is a snapshot of the financial position of a business at a point in time. It shows the assets, liabilities and capital of a business.

→ The trial balance is a useful starting point in the preparation of the financial statements. Adjustments to the trial balance are normally made before financial statements are prepared, e.g. accruals, prepayments, closing inventory and depreciation.

→ An inventory valuation is necessary for the preparation of financial statements.

→ Depreciation is the spreading of the cost of non current assets over a number of years

Next steps

Write out the main expenses in your business. Think about how to group the expenses in categories which might be useful in preparing an income statement. Try to think of the best layout of the income statement for your business.

This chapter concentrated on the financial statements of simple business format (a sole trader). Before going to Chapter 7, try to think of any differences you might expect to see in financial statements of companies, for instance, new expense types in the income statement.

_____

_____

_____

_____

The income statement and balance sheet of a company

This chapter extends your knowledge of the income statement and balance sheet for sole traders to limited companies. The underlying techniques used in preparing the financial statements for companies are exactly the same as those for sole traders. However, accounting has many rules and regulations which are more often applicable to the preparation of financial statements of companies. Before getting on with the practical side of company financial statements, let's consider some of these accounting rules.

Company law

Limited companies, regardless of size or type, are regulated by various pieces of legislation. Collectively, the law on companies is often referred to as the Companies Acts. They lay down rules for many aspects of a limited company, and cover many volumes. For example, the Companies Acts specify the minimum number of shareholders required, the duties of company directors, and the frequency of general meetings of a company.

The Companies Acts also contain a number of items relating to the format and content of financial statements. The Acts typically describe the minimum items which must be shown in financial statements. These minimum items depend on whether the company is small, medium or large. The size of the company is determined by a combination of the value of its assets, its turnover and the number of its employees, with the Acts defining what these values are.

All companies must make their financial statements available to the public by publishing them. Publication is normally achieved by filing the required financial statements at a Registrar of Companies (called Companies House in the UK). The exact publication requirements will vary by jurisdiction but, for example, a small company might only have to publish a summarised balance sheet; a medium-sized company might publish a more detailed balance sheet and a summarised income statement; while a large company would have to publish full details. In addition, the Companies Acts require two further reports: (1) a directors' report, and (2) an auditors' report. These are detailed later.

Book-keeping and Accounts for Entrepreneurs

Finally, the Companies Acts may also require what are termed 'Notes to the Accounts'. These notes give additional information to explain figures in the income statement or balance sheet. These might include, details of directors' salaries, directors' shareholding and numbers/salaries of staff.

Accounting standards

Like most professions, the accounting profession has its own set of rules and regulations. These are called accounting standards.

Accounting standards typically provide: (1) guidance on how to treat certain items in the financial statements, and (2) additional details on certain items. The standards are numerous and often complex. To add to the complexity, until recently many countries maintained their own unique set of accounting standards. In 2004, however, the European Union adopted the accounting standards set by the International Accounting Standards Board (IASB). These standards (known as International Financial Reporting Standards or IFRS) are now used in the preparation of the accounts of public companies in all European Union member states. Private companies also have the option to use IFRS.

The combination of accounting standards and companies legislation can make for some complex work in the preparation of company financial statements. As an entrepreneur you do not need a detailed knowledge of these standards. What is important is for you to be able to understand and interpret the financial statements of a company.

Finally, the financial statements referred to from here on are the published financial statements of a company. Internally, a company is free to prepare its financial statements in any manner it wishes. Financial statements for internal use are often called management accounts as they are used for management decision-making purposes.

The income statement of a company

The income statement of a company is not too different from that of a sole trader. Companies are of course often more complex businesses than sole traders or partnerships. This means that the income statements (and balance sheet) may have some items which are not seen in the accounts of a sole trader. Let me explain some of these items before looking at an example.

First, directors' salaries and other remuneration will be present. Directors are the persons responsible for the day-to-day running of a business. They may or may not be shareholders, that is, owners of the company. Next, auditors' fees will be a normal expense. Auditors verify (i.e. audit) the financial statements of a company. An audit is required by company law. Sole traders and partnerships do not normally need an audit. Finally, the income statement also is likely to show a taxation charge. Companies pay corporation tax on their profits. This tax is shown as an expense in the income statement.

However, as we will see below, you will not actually see many expenses on the face of the income statement.

Let's look at the example now. For the purposes of illustration, I have created a fictional company called ABC plc. The layout of the income statement (and later the balance sheet) is in accordance with IFRS and company law which applies to UK public companies. Similar formats are used for private companies. If you look at the income statement of a public company on their website, you may find that the income statement has some slight variations, but it will maintain the basic format of this example.

Income statement of ABC plc for the year ended 31/12/2008

	£m
Revenue	20,992
Cost of sales	(14,715)
Gross profit	6,227
Operating costs	(4,191)
Operating profit	2,086
Finance costs	(416)
Finance revenue	170
Share of associates profit	64
Profit before tax	1,904
Income tax expense	(466)
Profit for the financial year	1,438
Attributable to:	
Equity shareholders	1,430
Minority Interests	8

As you can see, the income statement is very brief. Let me explain some items. Revenue is simply the revenue generated from the operations of the company, in other words, sales. Cost of sales is the same as for a sole trader, as is gross profit. Expenses are simply totalled under the heading of 'Operating costs'. Finance costs and finance revenues are expenses such as interest paid and received. Share of associates profit is something which you will see in a group income statement, that is, the combined income statement of a group of companies (most large public companies are groups of companies). An associate is a company in which a group of companies has a substantial stake, but not outright control. This usually means more than 20 per cent but less than 50 per cent. More than 50 per cent would give the group control and make it a subsidiary company. The 'Income tax expense' amount refers to the taxation payable on the profits of the company.

The last two items show the amount of the profit which is attributable to the shareholders and what are termed Minority interests. In a large group of companies, the parent of the group may not own 100 per cent of its subsidiary and associate companies. When the financial statements of a group of companies are prepared, It is assumed that all associated and subsidiary companies are 100 per cent owned. This makes the adding together of income and expenses a lot easier. Then, the accounts are adjusted to show the portion of profit (in the income statement) and ownership (in the balance sheet) which are owned by minority interests.

You are probably asking yourself whether the income statement of a company is that simple. Yes, it is. However, much more information is given in what are called the 'Notes on the Financial Statements'. For example, a breakdown of operating costs might be shown on a note as follows:

	£m
Selling and distribution costs	2,675
Administrative expenses	1,474
Other operating expenses	58
Other operating income	(16)
Total	4,191

Still not very detailed, but that is all that is required under the accounting standards and company law. The notes on the financial statements give an increased amount of detail on all the financial statements. They are an integral part of the annual report (covered later in this chapter). For example, if you look at the annual report of British Airways (**www.britishairways.com**), you'll see the annual report for 2007–2008 has 4 pages of financial statements, but 46 pages of accompanying notes. All such notes are required by an accounting standard or by company law. The purpose of these notes is to provide the user (normally defined as an investor) with sufficient information about the company to make an informed investment decision.

The balance sheet of a company

The balance sheet of a company takes a similar format to that of a sole trader (have a look back at Figure 6.5 on page 100). As with the income statement, there are a number of items normally found on a company balance sheet that are not found on the balance sheet of a sole trader. Take a look at the sample for ABC plc on the next page.

As was the case with the income statement, this balance sheet is not too detailed. Again, the notes to the accounts will provide much more detail. You can see that the balance sheet has three major headings: assets, liabilities and equity. Equity is a similar concept to the capital of a sole trader.

In other words

Equity capital is money invested in a company that is not repaid to investors in the normal course of business. It usually represents the amount of money paid for shares by investors.

I will return to the equity section of the balance sheet later. First, let's see what kinds of assets and liabilities are on the balance sheet of ABC plc.

Balance sheet of ABC plc as at 31/12/2008

	£m
ASSETS	
Non-current assets	
Plant, property and equipment	8,226
Intangible assets	3,692
Investments in associates	1,112
	13,030
Current assets	
Inventories	2,226
Trade receivables	3,199
Cash and cash equivalents	1,333
	6,758
Total assets	19,788
EQUITY	
Equity share capital	187
Preference shares	1
Share premium	2,420
Retained income	5,346
	7,954
Minority Interest	66
Total equity	8,020
LIABILITIES	
Non-current liabilities	
Loans and borrowings	5,928
Deferred income tax	1,312
Trade and other payables	141
Provisions for liabilities	406
	7,787
Current liabilities	
Trade and other payables	2,956
Current income tax	244
Loans and borrowings	570
Other liabilities	211
	3,981
Total equity and liabilities	19,788

Assets

The assets on a company balance sheet are, like those of a sole trader, split into non-current and current. The only difference in company balance sheets is that accounting regulations specify that these specific headings be used, whereas in a sole trader's balance sheet we could use the term fixed assets instead of non-current assets, for example. Looking first at the non-current assets, you will see terms that I have not used before, which I will now explain.

Plant, property and equipment

Accounting regulations do not require a company to show anything more that one figure for all its physical assets, that is, plant, property and equipment. A note to the accounts is required, though, which shows the opening balance for each class of asset, additions, disposals and, of course, the depreciation figure.

Intangible assets

Non-current assets are often termed tangible assets as they are something we can see and touch. Intangible assets are assets which are not physical in nature but nonetheless can deliver future economic benefits. The most common intangible asset is goodwill.

In other words

Goodwill occurs when one business buys another. It is the amount of money over and above the book value of the net assets of a firm that a buyer is willing to pay.

Thinking back to Chapter 5, here's how goodwill would be accounted for in the general ledger. Assume I pay £7.5m for a business which has net assets totalling £6m. I am willing to pay over the odds by £1.5m because I know the business has built up a good reputation over the years. Assuming the purchase price of £7.5m is paid in cash, the ledger entries would be something like this:

Debit: Plant, property and equipment £6m

Debit: Goodwill £1.5m

Credit: Bank £7.5m

The balance sheet after the purchase of the new business will thus show goodwill as an intangible asset with a value of £1.5m. A final point on goodwill is that only *purchased* goodwill (i.e., the £1.5m in the example) can be included in a balance sheet. It is not permitted under accounting regulations to value the goodwill of a business and place it on a balance sheet.

Investments in associates

An associate company is one which is more than 20 per cent but less than 50 per cent owned by another. Ownership of 50 per cent or more implies a company is a subsidiary company. The term parent company is often used to describe the company which owns the subsidiary. Ownership is generally defined as holding ordinary shares which carry voting rights (this is covered in more detail later). Companies will normally invest in or buy other companies with a longer term view. Therefore, an investment in an associate company is shown under non-current assets as it is expected to be held for more than one year. If the investment is in a subsidiary company, the assets and liabilities are added to the assets and liabilities of the parent in the balance sheet and, likewise, the income and expenses are added together in the income statement.

Current assets

Looking at the current assets of ABC plc, these are quite similar to those we have seen in a sole traders' balance sheet. The only term not used before is *cash and cash equivalents*. This simply refers to cash held at the bank and other short-term deposits. It is a term recommended by accounting standards.

Equity

In Chapter 6, the owner's interest in a business was called capital. In a public or private company the owners are the shareholders. More specifically, holders of ordinary shares are the owners.

In other words

An **ordinary share** (in the US known as common stock) gives the holder partial ownership of a company. Holders of ordinary shares are entitled to voting rights in proportion to their holding.

As ordinary shareholders have voting rights they are entitled to attend the annual general meeting (AGM) of a company. An AGM is a gathering of the directors and shareholders of every company, required by law to be held each calendar year. Generally, not more than 15 months are allowed to elapse between two AGMs, and a 21-day written notice of the meeting date is required to be given to the shareholders. The main purpose of an AGM is to comply with legal requirements (company law), such as the presentation and approval of the audited accounts, election of directors, and appointment of auditors for the new accounting term. Other items that may also be discussed include compensation of officers (i.e., directors) and confirmation of any proposed dividend (a dividend is a share of profits).

As mentioned in Chapter 4, only public companies can issue shares to the public. The sale of ordinary shares is shown in the balance sheet as equity share capital – a total of £187m in the balance sheet of ABC plc. Ordinary shareholders may be paid a return called a dividend, but there is no right to any return. Preference shares, on the other hand, give a fixed return.

In other words

A **preference share** is a share which pays a regular and fixed return. Preference shareholders have a claim on the profits of a company before ordinary shareholders. Normally, preference shares do not carry any voting rights.

A preference share might, for example, give an 8 per cent payment each year to shareholders. The balance sheet of ABC plc shows £1m worth of preference shares, which relatively is a lot less than the equity share capital. This is quite typical, as companies don't want to commit to high fixed interest payments.

Shares are issued at their nominal (or par) value, which might be £1 for example. Investors might be willing to pay a lot more than this price as they will take account of both the past and future performance of the company. In accounting, shares are always shown in the balance sheet at nominal value. Any additional amount received is shown as a share premium. For example, in ABC plc the share premium is £2,420m, which is quite a bit more than the £188m in equity and preference shares. It is not unusual to see a large share premium in the balance sheet of a successful public company as shareholders are willing to pay over the odds in the hope of obtaining a good return through increasing share price on the stock market.

Retained income is also shown under the equity heading. This is simply the profits which have been kept in the company. When a company makes a profit it can choose to pay some, all, or none of the profit to shareholders as a dividend.

In other words

A **dividend** is a distribution of a company's profit, paid to shareholders. Usually dividends are paid out on a quarterly or six-monthly basis in cash. The amount of any dividend is determined by a company's board of directors.

The level of dividend paid varies widely from company to company. For example, Ryanair plc, a European low cost airline, vows never to pay a dividend, whereas GlaxoSmithKline, a global pharmaceutical company is known for paying high dividends. Any profits left after dividends are paid are accumulated and shown in the balance sheet. This is similar to the way profits of a sole trader are added to the capital account (see Chapter 6).

The final item shown in ABC's balance sheet is minority interest. The minority interest shown in the balance sheet is to reflect the assets which belong to other investors.

In other words

Minority interest is an accounting concept that refers to ownership of a subsidiary company that is less than 50 per cent and belongs to other investors.

Liabilities

As with a sole trader, liabilities are also split between non-current and current. As you can see in the balance sheet of ABC plc, trade payables and bank loans are shown. They are divided between non-current and current depending on when they are due for payment – that is, within one year or after one year. There are some other items which I will explain.

Deferred income tax

As the name suggests, deferred income tax is tax for which payment has been deferred until later. This is often caused by differences in how profits are calculated for taxation purposes compared to accounting. For example, it may be possible to reduce profits for taxation purposes by the full amount invested in new plant or equipment. This means that the tax liability is greatly reduced. Here's a simple example.

Assume a company buys an asset for £1,000 and depreciates it over five years on a straight-line basis. For taxation purposes, the same asset can be depreciated by 25 per cent on a reduced-balance basis. Taxation is 20 per cent.

Year end	Year 1	Year 2	Year 3	Year 4
Accounting value	800	600	400	200
Tax value	750	563	422	316
Temporary difference	50	37	(22)	(116)
Deferred liability/(asset) at 20%	10	7	(4)	(23)

In the above example, in Years 1 and 2, the tax depreciation is greater than the accounting depreciation, so there will be additional tax to be paid in the future which is recognised as a liability. In Years 3 and 4, the opposite is the case, so tax will be refunded.

Provisions for liabilities

According to accounting regulations, a provision is a liability of uncertain timing or amount. For example, if a company gives a warranty on its products it is likely at some time to have to repair or replace products under the warranty. The exact timing and amount of any warranty claims are not certain, but nonetheless a provision should be made in the accounts. If you remember back to Chapter 1, making such a provision is applying the prudence concept.

Current Income tax

The liability of income tax shown on the balance sheet of ABC plc is simply the amount of tax owed to the taxation authorities. As taxation is calculated based on profits at the accounting year end, a liability will exist in the balance sheet until it is paid.

The annual report

If you look at the website of any public company or large private company you will normally be quickly able to find the company's annual report. It is often under the 'Investor Relations' link. So before reading the rest of this section, why not go to the website of any company with which you are familiar and see if you can find the most recent annual report.

An annual report of a company is a document presented to shareholders at the annual general meeting (AGM). The precise contents of an annual report vary from company to company, but there are a number of common items which I outline below. One of the most important features is the financial statements and notes, which have been detailed already.

Business review

The annual report generally contains a section which reviews the operations of the company. For example, the 2008 annual report for Marks and Spencer plc gave a review of operations on the following operating sections: womenswear, menswear, kidswear, home, food, M&S Direct and also a review of operations separated as UK and International. The business review gives information on market conditions, sales growth, branding and plans for the future.

Financial review

Many annual reports give a one- or two-page summary of the main financial highlights for the year. A financial review might include summary data on revenue, profits, major costs, acquisitions and capital expenditure. Charts are often used to summarise data and make it more understandable to the general public.

Corporate governance

Corporate governance is the set of processes, customs, policies, laws, and institutions affecting the way a company is directed, administered or controlled. It also includes the relationships among the many stakeholders involved and the goals for which the corporation is governed.

In other words

A **stakeholder** is a party who affects, or can be affected by, a company's actions. Stakeholders include managers, employees, suppliers, customers, shareholders and the local community.

A report on corporate governance will include items such as details of the board of directors and their duties, directors' shareholdings, environmental policy, fairness to employees, and political donations.

Auditors' report

Under company law, the financial statements of a company must be audited (checked and verified) by an independent external auditor. An audit is an independent assessment of the fairness of the way a company's financial statements are presented by its management. It is performed by a competent, independent and objective person or persons, known as auditors, who then issue a report on the results of the audit. The auditors' report states whether or not the financial statements of the company are a fair representation of the underlying books of account.

Smaller companies may claim what is known as an audit exemption, if permitted under company law. This does not, however, remove the need to produce financial statements.

To summarise, while the financial statements are a large part of an annual report, the report includes other items. Most public companies now publish their annual report on the company's website.

Key points

→ In general terms, company financial statements are similar to those of any other form of business.

→ There are some new items, including expenditure, assets and liabilities that are unique to companies.

→ The equity capital of a company consists of share capital and retained profits.

→ In a group of companies, it is unlikely that all subsidiary companies are 100 per cent owned, and therefore a minority interest may exist.

→ The annual report of a company includes the financial statement and many other useful features which are of interest to investors.

Next steps

To familiarise yourself with the annual report of a company, choose four or five companies you know or find interesting. Go to their websites and download the most recent annual reports. They are often available in both PDF and web-page formats. Have a read through them and try to relate them back to the knowledge you have acquired in this chapter. Also, note any new items you find in the income statement or balance sheet and see if you can understand the notes to the accounts.

Cash flow statements

Cash is king. ALEX SPANOS (US real estate developer and self-made billionaire)

In Chapter 2, I stressed the importance of cash to a business, and the need to prepare a cash budget to ensure no cash shortfalls occur. The income statement and balance sheet, while including some cash, also include many items which are not necessarily cash. For example, trade receivables are the amount of money owed from customers at the end of the year and are a current asset. It is not the amount of cash received from customers, rather the amount to be received in the future. In the income statement, too, there are a number of items which are not cash, for example depreciation, accruals and prepayments.

As neither the income statement nor the balance sheet actually tells us a great deal about the cash flowing into and out of a business, a further financial statement is prepared called simply the 'cash flow statement'. According to accounting regulations, only limited companies need prepare cash flow statements. They might still be useful to other business types. The remainder of this chapter gives you the basics of preparing a cash flow statement and what the accounting regulations say. It is unlikely that you will ever prepare a cash flow statement yourself, as normally accountants or auditors do this. Nonetheless, understanding the cash flow statement is useful as it identifies the sources and uses of cash in a business.

Sources and uses of cash

The basic purpose of a cash flow statement is to show where a business generated cash and what cash was used for. The main sources and uses of cash can be identified as below:

	Cash sources	Cash uses
1	Profits	Losses
2	Sales of assets	Purchases of assets
3	Decrease in inventory	Increase in inventory
4	Decrease in receivables	Increase in receivables

5 Share capital issued	Dividends
6 Loans received	Loans repaid
7 Increase in payables	Decrease in payables

I'll explain each briefly.

1 Profits bring cash into the business, losses the opposite. Profit is not necessarily 100 per cent cash, but we'll deal with that later.

2 A sale of a non-current asset brings in cash, while a purchase requires cash to be paid out.

3 If inventory decreases, this means that in the normal course of business it is being sold and turned into cash. If it increases, cash is tied up in inventory

4 If receivables decrease, this means your customers have paid you cash, and the opposite if receivables increase

5 Issuing new shares for cash is a source of cash for a company. Dividends paid to shareholders is a use of cash.

6 If a company raises finance through a bank loan, this is a source of cash. Likewise, cash can be used to reduce or repay loans.

7 If the payables increase, cash is retained in the business rather than paid to suppliers. A decrease means suppliers have been paid using cash.

A cash flow statement tries to explain the increase or decrease in cash over the financial year. Therefore, starting with the cash balance at the beginning of the year, sources of cash are added and uses of cash subtracted to give the closing cash balance. Put another way, the cash flow statement should be able to explain the difference in the cash balances on the balance sheet between one year and the previous year.

Constructing the cash flow statement

There are two basic ways to prepare a cash flow statement. First, the *direct method* uses the exact cash flows (in and out) of a business. This might sound easy, but remember how the double-entry system of accounting works. All transactions are recorded according to the accruals concept (as explained in Chapter 1) and not when cash is paid. Therefore, rather than keep a second set of 'cash' records, most businesses use an *indirect method*. This means using the existing records and financial statements to indirectly derive the cash flows. This normally means using the income statement and balance sheet. Let's use an example to see how this works.

Below are summarised balance sheets of a company for two years.

Balance sheet as at 31 May

	2008	*2009*
	£m	*£m*
Non-current assets at cost	160	230
Accumulated depreciation	(60)	(90)
	100	140
Inventory	29	54
Bank and cash	7	22
	136	216
Equity and liabilities		
Share capital	55	71
Share premium account	9	13
Retained profits	45	95
Payables	27	37
	136	216

If we look at each item on these balance sheets we can see what has happened from 2008 to 2009:

→ The cost of fixed or non-current assets went up by £70m, which suggests we purchased some new assets.

→ The depreciation on assets was £30m (90–60) in 2009.

→ Inventory went up by £25m, tying up cash.

→ The bank (i.e. cash) balance increased by £15m.

→ Share capital increased by £16m, suggesting shares were issued for cash. Share premium increased by £4m, too, meaning the total cash from the share issue was £20m.

→ Retained profits went up by £50m, suggesting cash flows from profit.

Now we can prepare a simple cash flow statement, showing our sources and uses of cash.

Cash flow statement for the year ended 31 May 2009

	£m
Cash inflows	
Profit for the year (95–45)	50
Depreciation charges (90–60)	30
Funds generated from trading	80
Issue of shares (incl. share premium)	20
Increase in payables	10
	110
Cash outflows	
Purchases of fixed assets	(70)
Increase in stock	(25)
	(95)
Increase in cash	15

Note how the profit is adjusted for depreciation by adding it back. The retained profit is after depreciation and, as depreciation is not a cash flow (it's an accounting adjustment), it is added back to work out the amount of cash received from trading.

The example above gives the basics of how to prepare a cash flow statement from the balance sheet and/or income statement. Before I explain how a cash flow statement is prepared under accounting standards, let's examine in more detail how to derive the cash flow from trading, more correctly termed 'cash from operating activities'. When calculating the cash flow from operating activities we begin with the profit per the income statement and adjust for the effects of certain items, which I outline in the following paragraphs.

The effect of depreciation on cash flow

As we have seen in the example above, depreciation needs to be added back to profit because (1) the profit per the income statement will be after any depreciation charge, and (2) depreciation is not a cash flow. In Chapter 6 I explained how depreciation works, but when an asset is sold, the depreciation charge often needs to be adjusted, too.

For example, let's say a machine originally cost £30,000 and has been depreciated by £15,000, giving a net book value of £15,000. Now suppose the machine is sold for £16,000 cash. The cash received will be included in the cash flow statement. In addition, there is a profit on sale of £1,000 as the asset was sold for more than the book value. This £1,000 profit is shown on the income statement as a profit on the sale of assets. Another way to think about this is that £1,000 too much depreciation was charged. Likewise, a loss on the sale of a non-current asset means not enough depreciation was charged. As a profit or loss on the sale of an asset is really a depreciation adjustment, the amount would be added back (loss) or deducted (profit) from the operating profit when determining cash flows.

The effect of inventory on cash flow

At the end of a financial year, most companies will have inventories of raw materials or finished goods. Inventory, as you know, is a current asset and the value of closing inventory also has reduced the cost of sales in the income statement. Buying inventory does require cash, which means cash flows out of the business. In the cash flow statement, it is assumed all stock is paid for (see payables later). Thus, if inventory value increases, cash flows out, meaning that the cash flow is less than profit. The reverse applies if inventory value decreases.

The effect of receivables on cash flow

Most sales are on credit, which means cash flow will occur at some future date after the date of sale. Let's assume at the beginning of a year your company is owed £15,000 from customers. Your sales are £100,000, expenses £80,000, thus giving an operating profit of £20,000. Assuming no other adjustments to profit, the cash flow at the end of the year would be £35,000 (£20,000 + £15,000). Now suppose you were owed £30,000 by your customers at the end of the year. The cash flows would now be the £35,000 as before, but less £30,000 still owed, making it £5,000. A quicker way to work this out is to look at the increase or decrease in the amounts owed (receivables). In this example, the total amount owed increases by £15,000, which is cash tied up or, in other words, cash flows out. So, an increase in receivables is a cash outflow and will reduce the cash from operating activities, while a decrease will increase it.

The effect of payables on cash flow

Probably the best way to think of the effect of changes in amounts owed (payables) is to consider them as being the opposite of receivables. In other words, an increase in payables is equivalent to a cash inflow since we are effectively getting cash from suppliers by not paying them. A decrease in payables is the opposite and is equivalent to a cash outflow.

The effects of inventory, receivables and payables on cash flows are picked up from the balance sheet. As in the earlier example, we need a balance sheet for two consecutive years to be able to identify these increases or decreases in each. The cash flow statements we have looked at so far are not the same as what companies actually prepare. The next section explains what the accounting regulations require. However, the basic principle stands: a cash flow statement simply shows the cash inflows (sources of cash) and outflows (uses of cash) for a period of time.

The cash flow statement per accounting standards

International Accounting Standard 7 (IAS7) gives detail on the classifications of cash inflows and outflows to be used when preparing a cash flow statement. The examples up to this point have not classified cash sources or uses in any way. IAS7 specifies three classifications of cash flows:

1 cash flows from operating activities;
2 cash flows from financing activities;
3 cash flows from investing activities.

FIGURE 8.1

Cash Flow Statement of BB plc for the year ended 31/12/2008

		£m
Cash flows from operating activities		
Cash generated by operations	(Note 1)	4,099
Interest paid		(410)
Taxation paid		(346)
Net cash from operating activities		3,343
Cash flows from investing activities		
Acquisition of subsidiary companies		(169)
Purchase of plant, property and equipment		(3,442)
Proceeds from sales of plant, property and equipment		1,056
Dividends received		216
Increase in short term investments		(615)
		(2,954)
Cash flows from financing activities		
Proceeds from issues of shares		154
Increase in borrowings		9,333
Borrowings repaid		(7,593)
Dividends paid		(1,482)
		412
Net increase/(decrease) in cash		801
Cash at beginning of year		987
Cash at end of year		1,788

Note 1

	£m
Profit before tax	2,791
Depreciation	992
Profit on sale of assets	(188)
Increase in inventories	(276)
Increase in receivables	(71)
Increase in payables	851
Cash generated by operations	4,099

Figure 8.1 shows an example cash flow statement based on IAS7. As you can see, the cash flows are simply grouped according to the mentioned classifications. Why these three classifications? The amount of cash flows arising from operating activities is obviously a key indicator of the performance of the operations of a business. Having cash from operations reported shows whether a company has enough cash to pay loans, dividends and make investments. A separate classification for cash from investing activities is useful as this represents investment in possible future sources of cash, for example, new non-current assets or acquiring subsidiaries. Finally, cash flows from financing activities help providers of finance assess ability to take additional claims on cash, such as the ability to repay loans.

With the classifications of cash flows under IAS7, users of financial statements have the information needed to assess the ability of a company to generate cash. Many decisions taken by investors, for example, will be based around the ability of a company to generate cash flows. Making such decisions is not immediately possible if you are using data from the income statement and balance sheet alone.

Benefits and drawbacks of the cash flow statement

In comparison to the income statement and balance sheet, many people find the cash flow statement easy to understand. Cash is cash; it is not subjective in any way. This is the greatest advantage of a cash flow statement. For example, when comparing two companies (which we will address directly in Chapter 9) accounting techniques like depreciation may be inconsistent: maybe one company uses 10 per cent straight line, whereas the other uses 20 per cent reducing balance on the same class of assets. If we look at the cash flow statement to see cash invested in new assets, the figures are more comparable. A further advantage is that, in reality, the survival of a company depends on its ability to generate cash and have it available as needed. Lenders, suppliers, and shareholders will use the cash flow statement to see if adequate cash is being generated to pay loans, payables and dividends.

There are drawbacks of cash flow statements, too. One is that IAS7 does allow flexibility in the classification of cash flows. For example, one company might classify dividends paid as an operating cash flow, while another might classify them as a financing cash flow. Another drawback is that cash flows can be erratic at times, making year-on-year comparisons difficult. For instance, there may be a lot of investing cash flows in one year and none for several years after.

Key points

→ Companies must prepare a cash flow statement.

→ A cash flow statement shows the sources and uses of cash.

→ Cash flow is not the same as profit.

→ A cash flow statement is often prepared indirectly from the income statement and balance sheet.

→ IAS7 provides classifications for cash flows on the cash flow statement.

Next steps

Using the same companies that you chose for the 'Next steps' in Chapter 7, have a look at their cash flow statements. See if you can make sense of where cash comes from and what it is used for. Are there any items which concern you? For example, is there a lot of cash flow in from borrowing?

_____

_____

_____

_____

Analysing and valuing a business

Part Three

Analysing financial statements

Now that you know how financial statements are prepared, the next step is to appreciate what they are telling us about a business. For example, you might want an answer to the following questions: (1) Can I earn a better return on my money by investing it elsewhere? or, (2) How is my business performing compared to competitors? You might also want to assess the financial state of a business you want to buy, which I detail more in Chapter 10. In accounting, it is possible to give answers to such questions by comparing and understanding financial statements. In essence, what we are trying to do is to make the numbers in the financial statements 'tell the story' of how the company is performing over time, and highlight any potential problem areas.

Comparing financial statements

As we saw in Chapter 7, published financial statements show two years' figures (i.e. comparatives) in the income statement and balance sheet. This is a requirement of accounting regulations. You might think that comparing this year's results with last year's (or results for earlier years) can provide a use trend over time, and it does. But there are some difficulties with this. The most obvious problem is that the figures are historic. Figures such as revenues might show a trend upwards, but prices generally rise due to inflation. So how relevant is it to say that revenues rose by 3 per cent when inflation is also 3 per cent? Revenues in real terms did not grow at all.

Another difficulty is that one figure on its own, or a trend in a figure, may give a false impression. Consider the following example:

	£m
Company A profit	10
Company B profit	20

Before reading on, jot down here which company you think is the most profitable.

If we consider the numbers only, Company B is the answer, as it has a greater profit. But this is misleading. You have to ask how much money (capital) was invested to achieve the profit. Now consider the following, which gives some additional information on the assets of each business.

	Profit £m	Assets £m
Company A	10	40
Company B	20	100

Now, by expressing the profit as a percentage of assets, it is easy to see the picture has changed. Company A makes a return (profit) of 25 per cent (£10m/£40m) on its assets, whereas Company B makes a return of 20 per cent (£20m/£100m). Thus, Company A, despite having half the profit levels in £s of Company B, is actually making more productive use of its assets.

A final difficulty in comparing financial statements is the fact that not all businesses are the same. For example, to compare the financial statements of an airline with those of a power generation company does not make a lot of sense as the underlying businesses are very different. Even within the same industry, comparisons can be tenuous. For example, both easyJet and British Airways are airlines, but each company operates on a very different business model. EasyJet operates on a low-cost, no-frills basis, whereas British Airways offers quality service and flexibility.

With knowledge of the limitations in comparing financial statements, we can now move on to seeing how financial statements can be used to paint a picture of a business. In Chapter 1, I noted the many users of accounting information, including business owners, lenders, customers, suppliers, tax authorities and potential investors. As I have highlighted earlier, comparing numbers, like profit, can be problematic. Therefore, to make some sense of financial statements, accountants, business owners, and investors frequently use what is often termed financial ratio analysis. By using ratios, it is possible to eliminate the problem of the scale of numbers (i.e. £1 as a percentage of £10 equals 10 per cent in the same way that £1m as a percentage of £10m is 10 per cent). These ratios are the subject of the remainder of the chapter.

Financial ratios

In order to get the full story of the position of a company, compare one year with another or compare with another company, financial ratios are calculated in three broad areas:

1 profitability;

2 efficiency and liquidity;

3 gearing and investment.

All three categories provide useful information to business owners and other users of the financial statements. To help you understand these financial ratios, I will use the income statement and balance sheet shown in Figure 9.1 to calculate and interpret ratios.

FIGURE 9.1

Trading, profit and loss account of Seare Systems plc

	31/12/2009		31/12/2008	
	£	£	£	£
Sales		483,800		424,400
Cost of Sales				
Opening inventory	54,400		47,700	
Purchases	139,300		129,000	
Closing inventory	(34,400)		(31,000)	
		159,300		145,700
Gross Profit		324,500		278,700
Distribution costs	10,600		10,000	
Administration expenses	53,600		49,200	
Finance costs	45,100		40,300	
		109,300		99,500
Net operating profit/(loss)		215,200		179,200
Taxation		(51,600)		(37,600)
Profit after tax		163,600		141,600
Dividends		(16,400)		(17,400)
Retained profits		147,200		124,200
Profits carried forward		194,100		106,000
Profits carried forward		341,300		230,200

(Note: all sales and purchases are on credit. Finance costs consist of loan interest)

Balance sheet of Seare Systems plc

	31/12/2009		31/12/2008	
	£	£	£	£
Assets				
Non-current assets		642,200		451,700
Current Assets				
Inventory	34,400		31,000	
Trade receivables	43,500		53,400	
Bank	56,800		47,800	
		134,700		132,200
		776,900		583,900

	776,900			583,900

Equity & Liabilities
Equity

Ordinary £1 shares	187,400		124,600		
Retained profits	341,300		230,200		
		528,700			354,800

Non-current liabilities

Long term loans		187,200			187,200

Current liabilities

Trade payables	46,300		30,900		
Other creditors	14,700	61,000	11,000		41,900
		776,900			583,900

In total, we will calculate eleven ratios, all of which are given in the table in Figure 9.2. As I explain each ratio, look at this table in relation to the financial statements in the previous figure. As you can see, the ratios calculated are based on two years of financial statements. In practice, you might want to look at longer-term trends to get a full picture and remove the possibility of any one-off blips.

FIGURE 9.2

Ratio Analysis for Seare Systems plc

Profitability ratios	31/12/2009		31/12/2008	
Return on Capital employed (ROCE) (%)				
$\dfrac{\text{Operating profit before interest} \times 100}{\text{Capital employed}}$	$\dfrac{260,300 \times 100}{715,900} =$	36.4%	$\dfrac{219,500 \times 100}{542,000} =$	40.5%
Profit Margin (%)				
$\dfrac{\text{Operating profit before interest} \times 100}{\text{Sales}}$	$\dfrac{260,300 \times 100}{483,800} =$	53.8%	$\dfrac{219,500 \times 100}{424,400} =$	51.7%
Asset Turnover (times)				
$\dfrac{\text{Sales}}{\text{Capital employed}}$	$\dfrac{483,800}{715,900} =$	0.68	$\dfrac{424,400}{542,000} =$	0.78
Gross profit margin (%)				
$\dfrac{\text{Gross profit} \times 100}{\text{Sales}}$	$\dfrac{324,500 \times 100}{483,800} =$	67.1%	$\dfrac{278,700 \times 100}{424,400} =$	65.7%

Profitability ratios		31/12/2009			31/12/2008	
Working capital (efficiency) ratios						
Inventory turnover (times)						
Cost of sales / Average inventory	$\dfrac{159{,}300}{34{,}400} =$		4.63	$\dfrac{145{,}700}{31{,}000} =$		4.70
Average credit period allowed (days)						
Trade receivables × 365 / Credit sales	$\dfrac{43{,}500 \times 365}{483{,}800} =$		32.8	$\dfrac{53{,}400 \times 365}{424{,}400} =$		45.9
Average credit period received (days)						
Trade receivables × 365 / Credit purchases	$\dfrac{46{,}300 \times 365}{139{,}300} =$		121.3	$\dfrac{30{,}900 \times 365}{129{,}000} =$		87.4
Solvency ratios						
Current ratio						
Current assets / Current liabilities	$\dfrac{134{,}700}{61{,}000} =$		2.21:1	$\dfrac{132{,}200}{41{,}900} =$		3.16:1
Liquid (Acid Test/Quick) ratio						
Current assets – inventory / Current liabilities	$\dfrac{100{,}300}{61{,}000} =$		1.64:1	$\dfrac{101{,}200}{41{,}900} =$		2.42:1
Gearing and investment ratios						
Debt/equity ratio						
Debt / Equity	$\dfrac{187{,}200}{528{,}700} =$		0.35:1	$\dfrac{187{,}200}{354{,}800} =$		0.53:1
Interest Cover (times)						
Operating profit before interest / Interest	$\dfrac{260{,}300}{45{,}100} =$		5.77	$\dfrac{219{,}500}{40{,}300} =$		5.45
Earnings per share (£)						
Profit after tax, interest and preference dividends / # of ordinary shares in issue	$\dfrac{163{,}600}{187{,}400} =$		0.87	$\dfrac{141{,}600}{124{,}600} =$		1.14
Price/Earnings (years)						
Market price per share / Earnings per share	$\dfrac{12.50}{0.87} =$		14.3	$\dfrac{10.20}{1.14} =$		9.0
Dividend cover (times)						
Profit after tax and preference dividends / Total ordinary dividend	$\dfrac{163{,}600}{16{,}400} =$		9.98	$\dfrac{141{,}600}{17{,}400} =$		8.14

Analysing profitability

The objective of profitability ratios is to give an indication of the return (profit) on the investment in a business. Before looking at some ratios, think about this question: What is the minimum return on investment in a business you would deem acceptable?

The answer to this question is not an easy one. Each entrepreneur or business owner may have their own outlook on the required return. Any expected return is related to risk. So, for example, deposit accounts give a low rate of return – the interest rate is normally quite low, but there is typically little or no risk attached. However, if you invest in the stock market you may gain a higher level of return, but the risk is much greater – anyone who invested in bank shares in late 2008 can testify to this.

So, back to the question I asked above. I think a reasonable answer might be a return something greater than the rate available from putting your money on deposit and more in line with the return from riskier activity like investing in the stock market. With this in mind, if we are to compare the profitability of a business to anything, we could consider the risk free deposit rate and the return available from other sources.

Now, for the profitability ratios. The first ratio is called Return on Capital Employed (ROCE) and is defined as follows.

$$ROCE = \frac{\text{operating profit before interest} \times 100}{\text{capital employed}}$$

In other words

Capital employed is the amount of money (capital) which is invested (employed) in a business. It can be calculated as total equity plus non-current liabilities or total assets (current and non-current) less current liabilities.

There is one potential problem with the ROCE, which is what capital employed figure to use. Normally, the year-end figure is used, but this is likely to be higher than the capital employed at the beginning of the year. Some companies use a simple average figure, taking the average of the capital employed at the start and end of the year. Others use a rolling average, which might be best in a highly seasonal business. Whatever capital employed figure is used is a matter of judgement, but the important thing is to be consistent from one year to another.

Danger!

While it does not matter which capital employed figure is used, consistency in use is important. This applies to all financial ratios used in this chapter, so be sure you keep any calculations consistent over time.

The ROCE tells us the return made on capital employed before any distributions of profits (e.g. taxation, dividends or interest). For Seare Systems (see Figure 9.2), the ROCE was 40.5 per cent in 2008 and 36.4 per cent in 2009. I think we can say this is quite a good return as it is well above any interest available on deposits and a rate which might compensate shareholders for any additional risk. Additionally, the ROCE might be compared with that of similar companies to see if they are making a comparable return.

While the ROCE is quite good, there has been a fall in the ratio year-on-year. So what caused this decline? To help explain this it is possible to break the ROCE into two components, which are called (1) profit margin, and (2) asset turnover. Essentially, these components isolate how the capital of the business generates profits. Capital is the money used to buy assets, which in turn generate sales, and sales subsequently generate profit. This raises two questions: (1) how profitable are sales? and (2) how well is capital generating sales? The first question is answered by the profit margin ratio, the second by asset turnover. Each is calculated as follows:

$$\text{Profit margin} = \frac{\text{operating profit before interest} \times 100}{\text{sales}}$$

Book-keeping and Accounts for Entrepreneurs

$$\text{Asset turnover} = \frac{\text{sales}}{\text{capital employed}}$$

The profit margin (often called Return on Sales) tells us how profitable every pound (£) of sales was. For Seare Systems, we can see the profit margin increased from 51.7 per cent to 53.8 per cent year-on-year (see Figure 9.2). This improved profitability is a good sign. Changes in the profit margin can generally be attributed to either increases/decreases in sales prices and/or lower/higher costs. Again, the trend of the profit margin over a longer period of time and comparisons against other companies in the same business sector might be useful.

The asset turnover tells how productive our capital employed is. It is normally expressed as a multiple of capital employed. Some companies may have highly productive capital employed, others not. Looking at Seare Systems, we can see the asset turnover is less than one each year, meaning that capital employed does not generate its own value in sales. This is not necessarily a bad thing, as it may be compensated for by a high profit margin – which is exactly the case for Seare Systems.

The asset turnover for Seare System has fallen from 0.78 times to 0.68, which indicates that capital has not been used as efficiently in 2009 as in 2008. Why is this? Well, we can't tell from the ratio itself. However, looking at the balance sheet (see Figure 9.1), we can see that the value of non-current assets increased by almost £200,000. It is possible that new plant or equipment has been purchased which has not yet realised its full potential.

Danger!

In the example above of the asset turnover I have guessed that new non-current assets may not yet be fully productive. This is only a guess and would need to be verified. As we continue through this chapter, I will offer possible interpretations for changes in ratios. These interpretations, while being reasonable, are not in any way definite. If you are analysing your own financial statements, you will know your business circumstances and will be able to give more definite interpretations. If it's another business you cannot be so sure.

If you are mathematically minded, you may have noticed that the profit margin multiplied by the asset turnover gives the ROCE. In Seare Systems for 2009 this is 53.8% × 0.68, which equals 36.4%.

It is possible to produce many more profitability ratios. One very common ratio is the Gross Profit margin, which is calculated as follows:

$$\text{Gross Profit margin} = \frac{\text{gross profit} \times 100}{\text{sales}}$$

The Gross Profit margin reflects how profitable a business is based solely on the costs of purchase or manufacture. In general, a particular business sector will have an average Gross Profit margin. For example, the margin in a restaurant might be quite high while a motor dealer typically works on a small margin. For Seare Systems, we can see from Figure 9.2 that the Gross Profit margin has increased from 65.7 per cent to 67.1 per cent. Therefore, linking back to the profit margin component of the ROCE, we can say that the increase in profit margin can in part be attributed to a better Gross Profit margin.

You can also calculate ratios for expenditure. I don't do any here, but you could calculate each expense as a percentage of sales. This might help you find the root causes of increases in costs which might have caused profits to fall. For example, if you calculate distribution costs as a percentage of sales, you can determine how efficient your distribution is. If you get more sales out of the same distribution costs, your distribution channels are being more effective.

Analysing efficiency, liquidity, and solvency

As we have seen in calculating the ROCE above, measuring how efficiently the assets of a business are employed is important. We can perform a more detailed analysis of the current assets of a business to see how well these are being managed. It is possible to calculate ratios to assess how well a business is managing its inventory, trade receivables and trade payables. In addition, a vital element of working capital is cash. I mentioned in Chapter 2 how important it is to budget for the cash requirements of a business. A business needs to ensure that its working capital (current assets less current liabilities) is managed correctly to ensure that there's not too much cash tied up in inventory or trade receivables, and that cash is available to pay suppliers as necessary. Therefore, how well working capital is managed determines the solvency and liquidity of a business.

Liquidity and solvency are related. If assets cannot be converted to cash, debts like loan repayments or payments to suppliers may not be met. To be unable to pays debts as they fall due means a business is insolvent, which quite often leads to the failure of the business.

If the components of working capital are managed well, liquidity and solvency issues should not arise. We can calculate a number of ratios which help determine the efficiency with which a business manages its working capital. These ratios provide indicators of the liquidity and solvency of a business.

Working capital management

We can calculate a ratio for each of inventory, trade receivables, and trade payables which help paint a picture of how well a business is managing its working capital. The first ratio is stock turnover, which is calculated as follows:

$$\text{Inventory turnover} = \frac{\text{cost of sales}}{\text{average inventory}}$$

This ratio tells us how many times a year inventory is sold. You might notice the bottom line says 'average inventory'. This might be a simple average of the inventory at the start of the year and the end of the year or a rolling average. The reason for using an average is to try to remove any seasonal variation.

Looking back at Seare Systems (Figure 9.2), the inventory turnover has remained relatively stable year-on-year at 4.6 and 4.7 times. Put another way, inventory remains in the business for 79 days on average (365 days per annum divided by 4.6 times). You might also notice that I have used the inventory values at the end of the year. This is because I would need three years' data to be able to calculate an average inventory level. Earlier, when calculating the ROCE, it was noted that there was more than one acceptable way of deriving a figure for capital employed. Here again, it is possible to derive an average inventory figure in more than one way, and it does not matter too much which method you use as long as you are consistent.

A downward trend in the inventory turnover figure may be an indicator of poor inventory control. For example, stores may be poorly organised or older stock not sold. Again, we cannot say this for certain from the figures but at least we can ask the question. Inventory turnover depends to a large extent on the type of business. For example, if I look at 2008 financial statements of a retailer like Sainsbury's (**www.jsainsburys.co.uk**), I get the following data:

$$\frac{\text{cost of sales}}{\text{inventory}} = \frac{£16,835m}{£681m}$$

This gives an inventory turnover of 24.7 times per year, or, on average, inventory is held for 14.7 days (365/24.7). This makes sense as Sainsbury's main business is in fast-moving consumer goods (FMCG). In comparison, if I look at the financial statements of Siemens, the global electronic and engineering company (**http:w1.siemens.com/investor/en/ index.htm**) for 2008, I get the following corresponding data:

$$\frac{\text{cost of sales}}{\text{inventory}} = \frac{£56,284m}{£14,509m}$$

This gives an inventory turnover of 3.87 times per year or, on average, inventory is held for 94.3 days (365/3.87). While Siemens do make some FMCG products, the majority of their business is in the provision of technologies for automation, transportation and industry. This example again highlights the need to be careful when comparing two businesses using ratio analysis. To compare Sainsbury's with Tesco would make a lot more sense.

The next useful ratio reflects how well trade receivables are managed:

$$\text{Average period of credit given} = \frac{\text{trade receivables} \times 365}{\text{credit sales}}$$

This ratio tells how many days' credit, on average, is given to customers. The top line is multiplied by 365 to give the answer in days. If you want it in months, multiply by 12 instead. Looking again at Figure 9.2, at Seare Systems the period of credit given has fallen from just under 46 days to just under 33 days. This may be a reflection of improved credit control (granting credit to customers and collecting money). Obviously the trend of this ratio is important. If the average period of credit is increasing, solvency may be affected. If it is decreasing, this may be a good thing, but bear in mind that sales might be lost if credit control is too tight. It may also be possible to compare the ratio with an industry average. In the UK, the average period of credit given is likely to be in the 45–60 days' range.

The final ratio to help interpret the management of working capital is the average period of credit taken. This is very like the previous one, except it relates to suppliers. It is calculated as follows:

$$\text{Average period of credit taken} = \frac{\text{trade payables} \times 365}{\text{credit purchases}}$$

One thing to note about this ratio is that it may not always be possible to obtain the credit purchases figure from published financial statements.

Danger!

If certain figures are not available from published financial statements, a substitute figure may be used. For example, cost of sales may be used as a substitute for credit purchases. When substitute figures are used be careful to be consistent and also recognise that resulting ratio calculations may not be as useful.

For Seare Systems, the credit purchases figure is available. Figure 9.2 shows that the average period of credit taken has increased dramatically from 87.4 days to 121.3 days. This could be seen as a sign of a problematic situation, as suppliers are being paid on average nearly 35 days later. But why is this you might ask? The other two working capital ratios (inventory turnover and days' credit given) have remained stable or improved, meaning that cash should be readily available. This might prompt you to think that Seare Systems is holding on to cash for longer, or has bought something that may have increased the monies owed to suppliers. While we cannot be 100 per cent certain, it would seem that the latter may be the reason. Relative to the previous year, trade payables have increased by more than 50 per cent, from £30,900 to £46,300 (see Figure 9.1). This may be due to a combination of increased sales (which requires increased purchases) and the purchase of non-current assets, which may have been bought on credit and still have amounts owing.

For Seare Systems, my best guess would be that the increase in average days' credit taken is a one-off blip, but again the trend over a longer time frame might tell a more accurate story. While most businesses do take credit, an increase in the period taken can be an indication of liquidity problems. To determine if this is so, you can also look at the inventory turnover and average period of credit given to see if the trend in these ratios also reflects a potential problem.

The previous paragraph has highlighted a key feature of using ratios to analyse financial statements, which is that you often need to consider ratios as inter-related and to use a group of ratios to give the full story. So if you are using ratios to analyse financial statements, think about how ratios may have knock-on effects on each other.

All three of the ratios mentioned can be combined to give what is termed the 'cash conversion cycle'. This is the days in inventory (which is derived from inventory turnover), plus days' credit given, minus days' credit taken, as shown in the diagram below:

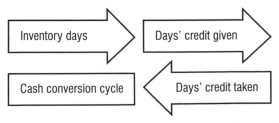

Again, the trend in the cash conversion cycle over time may be indicative of underlying management problems.

Solvency ratios

There are two ratios commonly used to help interpret quickly whether a business may have liquidity and/or solvency problems. The first one is called the Current ratio, and is calculated as follows:

$$\text{Current ratio} = \frac{\text{current assets}}{\text{current liabilities}}$$

The basic idea of this ratio is that for a company to be able to pay its debts as they fall due, current assets should cover current liabilities by some multiple. For Seare Systems, the ratio has declined quite a lot (see Figure 9.2) from 3.16:1 to 2.21:1. Looking again at the figures shown in Figure 9.1, it seems this decline can be explained by a larger relative increase in current liabilities – which, as we mentioned earlier, was mainly an increase in trade payables. So, is the Current ratio for Seare Systems acceptable? Generally a Current ratio of at least 2:1 is good. This means that current assets are twice current liabilities. So, even if some stock could not be sold or some trade receivables not paid, current liabilities would still probably be paid off. However, the 2:1 figure is only a guideline and must be taken in context.

Danger!

Any ratios which have suggested 'yardsticks' need to be taken in context. For example, the Current ratio has a suggested yardstick of 2:1, or the ROCE is often suggested as 15 per cent or better. However, such measures need to take into account the type of business.

For example, the Current ratio of Sainsbury's from their 2008 financial statements works out at 0.66:1, which is a bit below the 2:1 yardstick. This is not a problem as businesses like Sainsbury's tends to have low inventory, low receivables and high trade payables.

The second ratio used to assess liquidity/solvency is the Liquid ratio, and it is calculated as follows:

$$\text{Liquid ratio} = \frac{\text{current assets} - \text{inventory}}{\text{current liabilities}}$$

This ratio is also called the Quick ratio or the Acid Test ratio. It is very similar to the Current ratio, except that inventory is deducted from current assets. This is because inventory is traditionally regarded as being the least liquid current asset.

For Seare Systems, the Liquid ratio (shown in Figure 9.2) has also declined, from 2.42:1 to 1.64:1. The decline is quite similar to that in the Current ratio. As noted already, the declining Current ratio (and also now the Liquid ratio) can be explained by the relatively larger increase in current liabilities. A generally accepted yardstick for the Liquid ratio is at least 1:1, meaning that cash and trade receivables should equal current liabilities. Again, this yardstick needs to be treated with some caution and the industry/sector should be considered. Using the Sainsbury's 2008 financial statements, the Liquid ratio works out at 0.35:1, which might lead one to conclude that the company has liquidity problems. As an exercise, calculate the Current and Liquid ratios for other companies like Sainsbury's, such as Tesco or Morrisons.

The Current and Liquid ratios serve as useful indicators of the liquidity/solvency of a business. However, as with other ratios, the trend over time is important. It should be noted that a business may face short-term liquidity problems which could skew either of the above ratios. Short-term liquidity problems may arise as customers are slow to pay, or inventories are not being sold. Such problems are normally overcome through focused management of inventory and receivables.

Analysing gearing and investment

The final set of ratios are of interest to people who put money into a business: investors (shareholders) and lenders. While all ratios thus far are also important for providers of capital, there are several useful ratios which are particularly useful for this group.

First, let's look at two ratios which are particularly useful to lenders such as banks. A bank will be interested in two basic things: (1) how much existing debt the business has, and (2) whether repayments can be made. The former can be assessed by the Debt/Equity ratio, the latter by the Interest Cover ratio.

The Debt/Equity ratio is calculated as follows:

$$\text{Debt/Equity ratio} = \frac{\text{debt}}{\text{equity}}$$

Debt is long-term debt, which is normally taken to mean long-term bank loans and other debt finance found under the non-current liabilities heading in the balance sheet. Equity is the shareholders' equity, or the capital provided by or attributable to shareholders (share capital and accumulated profits). For Seare Systems, the Debt/Equity ratio has improved from 0.53:1 to 0.35:1 (or 53 per cent to 35 per cent). If you look at the figures in Figure 9.2, you can see that this improvement is due to the increased equity as the debt level remains stable. In general, if this ratio is greater than 1:1, then a business is said to be lowly-geared; less than 1:1 makes it highly-geared.

For a potential investor or lendor, the higher the level of gearing the more risky the business may be. From a potential shareholder's view, if more cash is needed to pay interest on debt, less is available for dividends. From a lender's view, if the level of existing debt is high, repaying any additional debt may be problematic. However, high gearing is not necessarily a bad thing. Once monies borrowed are put to good use and earn a return greater than the rate of interest paid, overall company profits grow. Managers use investment evaluation techniques to select investments (such as building a new production facility) which will produce good returns. Interestingly, the return sought from investments often uses the ROCE as a starting point.

The next ratio, Interest Cover, is useful to lenders in particular. It is calculated as follows:

$$\text{Interest Cover ratio} = \frac{\text{operating profit before interest}}{\text{interest}}$$

The Interest Cover ratio simply tells us how many times operating profit (before interest, tax and dividends) covers interest. From a lender's perspective, a higher level of interest cover is preferred. If the interest cover is low, then a business might have trouble meeting interest payment on borrowings, which certainly would not bode well for repayments of the principal (the amount borrowed).

Looking at the figure for Seare Systems, we can see that Interest Cover is hovering around 5.5 times in both years. This, combined with the low gearing above, would be a good sign for a potential lender.

While lenders are concerned with ensuring interest and principal are repaid, shareholders are in a somewhat similar way concerned with the ability of a business to generate profits which in turn may be paid as dividends. Even if dividends paid are not a very high proportion of profits, shareholders can sell their shares at a profit. Having said that, unless a company can show a history of good profits and convince the markets that future profits are likely, share prices are unlikely to rise. Thus, shareholders are concerned with both profitability and dividends. While ratios like the ROCE may be used by shareholders, there are a number of other ratios which they may find particularly useful.

Earnings per Share (EPS) represents the profit per individual share. It is calculated as follows:

$$\text{EPS} = \frac{\text{Profit after tax, interest and preference dividends}}{\text{\# of ordinary shares in issue}}$$

The top portion of the EPS ratio represents the profit that is available for payout as a dividend. This does not at all mean it will be paid out, but it is the profit available to ordinary shareholders. Given that the bottom portion of the EPS is the number of ordinary shares issued, the EPS is not very comparable between companies. However, the trend of the EPS of a particular company is a very important indicator of how well the company is performing and it is also an important variable in determining a share's price (see the Price/Earnings ratio next).

For Seare Systems, we can see from Figure 9.2 that EPS has fallen from £1.14 per share to 87p per share. Can you see why? Jot down why you think the EPS has fallen:

While earnings for Seare Systems have increased, the number of shares in issue has risen from 124,600 to 187,400. This highlights a potential problem in the EPS ratio in that the number of shares issued may vary from year to year. In practice, this is often overcome by using a weighted average number of shares issued over a year. This evens out the effect of new share issues.

The Price/Earnings (P/E) ratio shows a company's current share price relative to its current earnings. It is calculated as follows:

$$P/E \ ratio = \frac{market\ price\ per\ share}{earning\ per\ share}$$

Looking at Seare Systems, the P/E ratio has improved to 14.3 from 9.0. In general, a high P/E suggests that investors are expecting higher earnings growth in the future compared to companies with a lower P/E. However, the P/E ratio doesn't tell us the whole story. It's usually more useful to compare the P/E ratio of one company to that of other companies in the same industry, than to the market in general, or against the company's own P/E trend. It would not be useful for investors to compare the P/E of a technology company (high P/E) to a utility company (low P/E) since each industry has very different growth prospects. We will see the P/E ratio again in the next chapter.

Care should be taken with the P/E ratio because the bottom part of the ratio is the EPS, which, as stated above, may not be that comparable between companies. There are some crude yardsticks for the P/E ratio, as follows:

→ A P/E of less than 5–10 means that company is viewed as not performing so well.

→ A ratio of 10–15 means a company is performing satisfactorily.

→ A ratio above 15 means that future prospects for a company are extremely good.

Again, as with all such yardsticks, these may vary by industry and depend on other factors like the general economic environment.

In summary of this chapter, financial ratios may be used to assess the profitability, liquidity, solvency, efficiency, and capital structure of an organisation. We have seen that financial statements, while useful and informative, are not usually directly comparable. Financial ratios overcome this problem. Analysing an organisation using ratios does have limitations which have been outlined throughout the chapter. However, by analysing an organisation through a combination of financial statements and financial ratios, a lender, investor or supplier will obtain a reasonable picture of how a company is performing and whether it is managing its resources efficiently.

Key points

→ Financial statements are limited in that figures therein may not be
directly comparable with those of other companies.

→ Financial ratios can be used to overcome this problem and provide
a fuller picture of the performance of a business.

→ Ratios can be calculated to assess profitability, efficiency, solvency,
gearing and investment return.

→ Yardsticks provided for some financial ratios need to be treated with
care.

Next step

Using one company from the 'Next step' in Chapter 7, use your knowledge of financial ratios to analyse and interpret the financial statements.
Then look for another company in the same sector and do a similar
analysis.

_____

_____

_____

_____

Valuing a business

Chapter Ten

Having come to terms with the book-keeping and financial statement preparation aspects of accounting, things should run relatively smoothly for you. But, as I'm sure you know as an entrepreneur, the world does not stand still. With good management and some luck your business will grow over time. Business growth in itself does not make the accounting work more difficult, just higher in volume. Your need for information will no doubt grow and spread beyond the realms of income, expenditure, and profits.

As an entrepreneur, information on your business performance is always crucial. Once your first business is up and running you'll most likely seek out the next business adventure. Maybe you'll start another business; or, you could simply buy another business and develop it.

 Why not invest your assets in the companies you really like? As Mae West said, 'Too much of a good thing can be wonderful.' WARREN BUFFETT

Like any investment, buying a business is a big decision. Even if you like the business you want to buy, many factors need to be considered: the location, market, cost structure, existing management and product portfolio, to name but a few. At the end of the day, the most important factor will be the price you pay. Pay too much and the future returns may not justify the cost; pay too little and you may find some skeletons in the cupboard which it will cost you to remedy. This chapter will provide you with some basic guidelines on how businesses can be valued, and give you the basic knowledge to assess if the price is right. The chapter will link back to material in Chapter 9 in some cases, so flick back if you need to.

Valuation basics

As we now know, the balance sheet of a company is a list of its assets and liabilities. Put another way, the balance sheet represents the value of a business. However, the value as depicted in the balance sheet is a historic value and does not take into account the future earnings of a business. This historic value is referred to as the 'book value' of a business, as it is the money value recorded in the books of account. For example, looking back at the balance sheet of Seare Systems plc in Chapter 9 (see Figure 9.1 on page 148), the book value of the business for 2009 is £528,700 – which is the book value of equity.

Business owners who wish to sell their business will usually ask for a price above the book value. There may be many reasons for this. Here are some examples:

→ Some assets in the business, such as land and buildings, may not be reflected in the balance sheet at their true market value.

→ A business owner may want to be compensated for loss of future earnings.

→ The business may have built up a loyal customer base over time, for which the owner wants to be compensated.

If a business is a public limited company, valuing it is relatively simple as you could use the market price of a share as a guideline. Without being too detailed, the price of any shares sold publically should incorporate all available information. Thus, if it is expected that a company will continue to be profitable, the market price of the share is likely to be higher than any book value. The term market capitalisation is used to describe the total market value of a public company. It can be calculated as follows:

Total market value = market price per share × number of shares in issue

Obviously, the market price can move up and down, drastically affecting the market value. Think of the declining market share price of many UK and global banks in late 2008 and early 2009.

If the company is private, things are a little more difficult as shares are not traded on any market. This does not mean that it is impossible to put a 'market value' on shares of a private company. In Chapter 9, we calculated the ROCE for Seare Systems in 2009 at 36.4 per cent. Let's assume Seare Systems is a private company. A potential investor or buyer of this business might say this is an extremely good return, and take 25 per cent as a good return on investment. What this investor is effectively saying is:

$$25\% = \frac{\text{profit before interest and tax}}{\text{market value}}$$

Plugging in the figure from Seare Systems for 2009, we can calculate the market value as:

$$\text{Market value} = \frac{260{,}300}{25\%}$$

This gives a value of £1,041,200. Dividing this by the number of shares (187,400) would give a value of £5.55 per share. Of course, another investor might require a higher or lower return which would affect the value of the company.

Valuation techniques

Business valuation techniques fall into the following categories, depending on what their major focus is. Possibilities include:

→ business assets;

→ historical earnings or cash flow;

→ a combination of assets and earnings;

→ the market for similar businesses, including comparable sales, industry rule of thumb, and P/E ratio methods;

→ future earnings.

I explain each below. For this portion of the chapter, I assume that the business to be valued is a private company.

Asset-based valuations

I have already described the concept of the book value of a business. You might think this is the minimum value for which you can buy a business. This may not be the case, though, as the liquidation value of a business may be less than the book value. Liquidation value is the amount that would be left over if you had to sell your business quickly, without taking the time to get the full market value, and then used the proceeds to pay off all debts. There's little point in going through all the trouble of negotiating a sale of your business if you end up selling for liquidation value – it would be easier to go out of business, and save yourself the time and costs involved in selling the business. Thus, liquidation value is not generally considered at all. It might be the floor price of a business, which can be used in negotiations.

Danger!

Book value, while possibly a better reflection of the value of a business than liquidation value, should be treated with some caution. A business owner might 'dress-up' the financial statements before showing them to a potential buyer. This is not to imply that anything illegal is taking place, rather the seller is trying to reflect what the financial statements might look like under a new owner. For example, in a family-run business, salaries of family members might be excluded from income statements or profit forecasts.

Earnings or cash-flow based valuations

This method has been shown earlier and is commonly used. It involves first determining a figure that represents the historical earnings (profits) of the company. This might be an average of the operating profits before interest and tax over previous years. For example, if the operating profit before interest and tax was £100,000 and the buyer required a return of 25 per cent, an earnings method would yield a price of £100,000/0.25 or £400,000.

An alternative is to use cash flows. The free cash flow of a business can be used as a starting point, which can be taken as the net increase in cash from the cash flow statement and adding back any interest paid. The resulting figure is the cash the business would have if debt free. Then, assuming the buyer of the business borrows money to complete the purchase, it is possible to determine the value of the business incorporating the buyer's expected return. Here's an example:

A business has free cash flow of £100,000 per year. A buyer is willing to buy this business using borrowings which will be repaid in five years,

This requires a minimum free cash flow of 5 × £100,000 = £500,000.

Now, let's assume the buyer requires a 20% annual return = £100,000 × 20% = £20,000 meaning that only £80,000 per year is available to make loan repayments.

An annual payment of £80,000 could support a five-year loan of approximately £346,300 at 5%, or £348,421 at 10% interest. These are effectively the business values.

(A very useful calculator for these types of calculation can be found at http://www.dinkytown.net/java/ComplexLoan.html)

Using the cash flow method above depends on the interest rate and loan repayment term available from a lender.

Combined asset and earning valuations

As you know both assets and earning valuation methods already, here's an example of a combined assets and earnings method.

Let's say the book value of a business per the balance sheet is £280,000. This is a minimum or base price.

Now let's assume that your historical annual earnings figure is £150,000. How much of this earnings figure is attributable to the assets? You might calculate that the ROCE (i.e. return on assets) is 10% under current market conditions Thus, earnings attributable to assets is £15,000. Subtracting this 'asset return' figure from your total earnings gives what is often termed 'excess earnings': £150,000 – £15,000 = £135,000.

Now suppose the required return is 20%. Using the excess earnings as a base for this return, the value of excess earnings is £675,000. Add to this the book value of your assets, and you arrive at a total price of £955,000.

The 'excess earnings' method is commonly used. A variant is to revalue balance sheet assets at current market value, which inevitably gives a higher value of the business.

Valuations based on similar businesses

Several valuation methods are based primarily on the market price for similar businesses at a given point in time. They may at least act as a benchmark value. Compared to the methods examined thus far, any market-based method can be a good reality check.

The comparable sales method attempts to use similar businesses, which have recently sold, as a basis for valuation. It may be possible to use the comparable sales figures to set a price for your business, adjusting appropriately for differences. While this idea is readily applicable to property sales, the method may be difficult to apply to business valuations because of problems in gathering information about business sales and because of the unique character of each business.

Rules of thumb/industry averages are another frequently used method. These are often based on experience and on published data for an industry. For example, the type of business you want to buy has been selling for about four times annual revenue. However, a rule of thumb does not take into account any of the factors that make a business unique, and using one can result in a price that's too high or too low. Nevertheless, small businesses are often sold at a price based on rule of thumb, simply because it's a relatively fast, cheap method to use, and because it will result in a price that seems reasonable based on sales of similar businesses.

In Chapter 9, we discussed the P/E ratio. P/E ratios of public companies or an industry are widely available – for example on **www.ft.com**. The P/E ratio of a public company can be used as a comparison for a private company. However, public companies are possibly less risky than a private company and can command a premium price. Also, if you buy a private company, it may be much harder to liquidate (sell) it than selling shares in a public company. For these reasons, using the P/E ratio of a public company should be treated with some caution. If you are to use a comparable P/E ratio to calculate a business value, you simply work out the earnings per share (as in Chapter 9) and multiply by the P/E ratio.

Valuation on future earnings

Theoretically, anyone purchasing a business is interested in the future of the business more than the past. Therefore, a valuation based on the company's expected earnings, discounted back to the value of money in today's terms, should be very close to answering the question about how much the business is really worth.

At least that's the theory. In practice, valuations based on future performance of the company are probably the most difficult to do because we must make estimates and projections. Nevertheless, it may be worth trying one of these methods. If carefully done, valuation methods based on future earnings can result in setting the highest reasonable price for a business.

Methods based on future earnings are frequently used by large organisations in merger or acquisition situations. So, how do you go about setting a price based on future earnings? The first step is to look at the financial statements. Working from these, you can create projected statements that extend for five or more years into the future. Each year's free cash flows or earnings can be determined. These projections should assume no major changes by a prospective buyer, since you are trying to measure the company as it exists today.

Once you have done this, the projected free cash flow (or earnings) from each year is discounted back to the present value of money, to arrive at what is called the net present value (NPV) of each cash flow. These NPVs are added up, to arrive at a total NPV of the company's earnings for the projected future.

How do you compute NPV? The easiest way is to look up what is called a present value table. There's one at this link: **http://www.sme-toolkit.org/smetoolkit/en/content/en/734/Present-Value-Table** or just Google for present value table. Below is an extract from a present value table.

Year	9.0%	9.5%	10.0%	10.5%
1	0.917	0.913	0.909	0.905
2	0.842	0.834	0.826	0.819
3	0.772	0.762	0.751	0.741

A present value table is read by looking at the year in which the cash flow occurs and the presumed rate of interest, or 'discount rate' as it is normally termed. For example, a cash flow of £10,000 in three years from now would be equivalent to £7,510 today if the discount rate is 10 per cent (£10,000 × 0.751). The key question is deciding which discount rate to use. The higher the rate, the lower the answer you'll get as to the value of the company. The discount rate must reflect a best guess as to what the market rate will be for investments of a similar nature over the next five years. It could also factor in a buyer's expected cost of capital (i.e. the interest rate on an acquisition loan). You might want to seek professional investment appraisal advice on which discount rate to use.

Let's say that after doing your best to look into the future and forecast the next three years' cash flow, you arrive at the figures shown in Figure 10.1. Assuming a 10 per cent discount rate, you come up with the present value figures as also shown in Figure 10.1.

FIGURE 10.1

Year	Cash flow	Discount factor	Present value
1	100,000	0.909	90,900
2	150,000	0.826	123,900
3	180,000	0.751	135,180
			349,980

Adding up the present values gives a net present value of £349,980. Now let's assume that the total value of net assets at the end of year 3 was £1,000,000. This equates to £751,000 in today's terms (£1,000,000 × 0.751). Therefore, we can say the value of the business using this method is £751,000 + £349,980, which is £1,100,980.

The NPV method is often cited as the most 'technically' sound method of evaluating future cash flows and therefore is used frequently. However, its biggest problem can be identifying and/or estimating those same cash flows.

Key points

→ Financial statements only portray the book value of a company.

→ The market value of a public company can be determined by reference to its share price.

→ The valuation of a private company can be more difficult. A value can be derived using book value as a starting point and then future cash flows and earnings can be examined.

→ Other valuation methods are possible, using comparisons to similar companies for which market data is available.

→ The present value of future cash flows using the NPV technique is probably the most technically sound method of valuing a business.

Web bonus

At our website, **www.forentrepreneursbooks.com**, click on the 'Book-keeping and Accounting for Entrepreneurs' button. Click on the link for Chapter 10, where you will find a link to a useful web tool which can help you calculate a business value based on projected cash flows.

Final words

I hope this book has given you a basic understanding of book-keeping and accounting. The best way to put the book to use is to practise what you have learned. Get your business working as well as you can for you by ensuring you have good and timely accounting information.

Additionally, see the website, **www.forentrepreneursbooks.com** for the bonus material specified in this book, as well as a blog written by all the authors in the 'for entrpreneurs' series of books. You may find the other titles in the series helpful as well. They include books on starting your business, growing your business, sales for entrepreneurs, and market-ing for entrepreneurs.

Glossary of accounting terms

Account: a section in a ledger devoted to a single aspect of a business (e.g. a bank account, wages account, office expenses account).

Accounting cycle: this covers everything from opening the books at the start of the year to closing them at the end. In other words, everything you need to do in one accounting year.

Accounting equation: the formula used to prepare a balance sheet: assets – liabilities = capital.

Accounts payable: an account in the nominal ledger which contains the overall balance owing to suppliers. The account might also be called 'Trade payables'.

Accounts payable ledger: a subsidiary ledger which holds the accounts of a business's suppliers. A single control account is held in the nominal ledger, which shows the total balance of all the accounts in the purchase ledger.

Accounts receivable: an account in the nominal ledger which contains the overall balance owed by customers.

Accounts receivable ledger: a subsidiary ledger which holds the accounts of a business's customers. A single control account is held in the nominal ledger, which shows the total balance of all the accounts in the sales ledger.

Accruals: if during the course of a business certain charges are incurred but no invoice is received, then these charges are referred to as accruals (they 'accrue' or increase in value) These items (or an estimate of their value) should still be included in the income statement.

Accumulated depreciation account: this is an account held in the nominal ledger, which holds the depreciation of a fixed asset until the end of the asset's useful life (either because it has been scrapped or sold). It is credited each year with that year's depreciation, hence the balance increases (i.e., accumulates) over a period of time. Each fixed asset will have its own accumulated depreciation account.

Amortisation: the depreciation (or repayment) of an (usually) intangible asset (e.g. loan, mortgage) over a fixed period of time. Example: if a loan of £12,000 is amortised over 1 year with no interest, the monthly payments would be £1,000 a month.

Assets: assets represent what a business owns or is due. Equipment, vehicles, buildings, creditors, money in the bank, cash are all examples of the assets of a business. Typical breakdown includes 'current assets' and 'non-current assets'.

Audit: the process of checking every entry in a set of books to make sure they agree with the original paperwork (e.g. checking a journal's entries against the original purchase and sales invoices).

Audit trail: a list of transactions in the order they occurred.

Balance sheet: a summary of all the accounts of a business. Usually prepared at the end of each financial year. The term 'balance sheet' implies that the combined balance of assets exactly equals the liabilities and equity.

Bill: a term typically used to describe a purchase invoice (e.g. an invoice from a supplier).

Books of prime entry: the first place that business transactions are recorded in a business.

Break-even: the point at which a business makes neither a profit nor a loss.

Called-up share capital: the value of issued but unpaid shares for which a company has requested payment. (See also Paid-up share capital)

Capital: an amount of money put into the business (usually by its owners) as opposed to money earned by the business.

Cash book: a journal where a business's cash sales and purchases are entered. A cash book can also be used to record the transactions of a bank account.

Cash flow: a report which shows the flow of money in and out of the business over a period of time.

Chart of accounts: a list of all the accounts held in the nominal ledger.

Closing the books: a term used to describe the journal entries necessary to close the sales and expense accounts of a business at year end by posting their balances to the profit and loss account, and ultimately to close the profit and loss account too by posting its balance to a capital or other account.

Companies House (UK only): the title given to the government department which collects and stores information supplied by limited companies. A limited company must supply Companies House with a statement of its final accounts every year (e.g. income statement and balance sheet).

Compensating error: a double-entry term applied to a mistake which has cancelled out another mistake.

Compound interest: interest applied on the capital plus all interest accrued to date. For example, a loan with an annually applied rate of 10% for £1,000 over two years would yield a gross total of £1,210 at the end of the period (year 1 interest=£100, year two interest=£110). The same loan with simple interest applied would yield £1,200 (interest on both years is £100 per year).

Control account: an account held in a ledger which summarises the balance of all the accounts in the same or another ledger. Typically each subsidiary ledger will have a control account which will be mirrored by another control account in the nominal ledger.

Cost of Goods Sold (COGS): a formula for working out the direct costs of your stock sold over a particular period. The result represents the gross profit. The formula is: opening stock + purchases − closing stock.

Cost of sales: a formula for working out the direct costs of your sales (including stock) over a particular period. The result represents the gross profit. The formula is: opening stock + purchases + direct expenses – closing stock. Also, see Cost of Goods Sold.

Credit: a column in a journal or ledger to record the 'From' side of a transaction (e.g. if you buy some petrol using a cheque then the money is paid from the bank to the petrol account, you would therefore credit the bank when making the journal entry).

Credit note: a sales invoice in reverse. A typical example is where you issue an invoice for £100, the customer then returns £25 worth of the goods, so you issue the customer with a credit note to say that you owe the customer £25.

Creditors: a list of suppliers to whom the business owes money.

Creditors (control account): an account in the nominal ledger which contains the overall balance of the Purchase ledger This is the same as the Accounts payable control account.

Current assets: these include money in the bank, petty cash, money received but not yet banked, money owed to the business by its customers, raw materials for manufacturing, and stock bought for resale. They are termed 'current' because they are active accounts.

Current liabilities: these include bank overdrafts, short-term loans (less than a year), and what the business owes its suppliers. They are termed 'current' for the same reasons outlined under 'current assets'.

Day books: see Books of prime entry.

Days Sales Outstanding (DSO): how long on average it takes a company to collect the money owed to it.

Debenture: this is a type of stock issued by a limited company. It is the safest type of stock in that it is really a loan to the company and is usually tied to some of the company's assets, so should the company fail, the debenture holder will have first call on any assets.

Debit: a column in a journal or ledger to record the 'To' side of a transaction (e.g. if you are paying money into your bank account you would debit the bank when making the journal entry).

Debtors: a list of customers who owe money to the business.

Debtors (control account): an account in the nominal ledger which contains the overall balance of the Sales ledger.

Depreciation: the value of assets usually decreases as over time. The amount or percentage it decreases by is called depreciation. This is normally calculated at the end of every accounting period (usually, a year). It is shown in both the income statement (charge for the year) and the balance sheet (accumulated depreciation) of a business.

Dividends: these are payments to the shareholders of a limited company.

Double-entry book-keeping: a system which accounts for every aspect of a transaction – where it came from and where it went to. This from-and-to aspect of a transaction (called crediting and debiting) is what the term double-entry means.

Drawings: the money taken out of a business by its owner(s) for personal use. This is entirely different from wages paid to a business's employees, or the wages or remuneration of a limited company's directors (see Wages).

EBIT: earnings before interest and tax (profit before any interest or taxes have been deducted).

EBITA: earnings before interest, tax and amortisation (profit before any interest, taxes or amortisation have been deducted).

EBITDA: earnings before interest, tax, depreciation and amortisation (profit before any interest, taxes, depreciation or amortisation have been deducted).

Entry: part of a transaction recorded in a journal or posted to a ledger.

EPS: earnings per share.

Equity: the value of the business to the owner of the business (which is the difference between the business's assets and liabilities).

Equity capital: money invested in a company that is not repaid to customers in the normal course of business (often paid for shares).

Error of commission: a double-entry term which means that one or both sides of a double-entry has been posted to the wrong account (but is within the same class of account). Example: Petrol expense posted to Vehicle maintenance expense.

Error of omission: a double-entry term which means that a transaction has been omitted from the books entirely.

Error of original entry: a double-entry term which means that a transaction has been entered with the wrong amount.

Error of principle: a double-entry term which means that one (or both) sides of a double-entry has been posted to the wrong account (which is also a different class of account). Example: Petrol expense posted to Fixtures and fittings.

Expenditure: goods or services purchased directly for the running of the business. This does not include goods bought for resale or any items of a capital nature.

Fixtures and fittings: this is a class of non-current asset which includes office furniture, filing cabinets, display cases, warehouse shelving and the like.

FMCG: fast-moving consumer goods.

Gearing: the comparison of a company's long-term debt compared to its assets.

Goodwill: this is an extra value placed on a business if the owner of a business decides it is worth more than the value of its assets. It is usually included where the business is to be sold as a going concern.

Gross margin: the difference between the selling price of a product or service and the cost of that product or service often shown as a percentage. If a product sold for £100 and cost £60 to buy or manufacture, the gross margin would be 40%.

Gross profit: sales less cost of sales, assuming sales is greater than cost of sales.

IASB: International Accounting Standards Board.

IFRS: International Financial Reporting Standards.

Imprest system: a method of topping up petty cash. A fixed sum of petty cash is placed in the petty cash box. When the petty cash balance is

Glossary of accounting terms

nearing zero, it is topped up back to its original level again (known as restoring the Imprest).

Income: money received by a business from its commercial activities. See Revenue.

Inland Revenue: the government department usually responsible for collecting your tax. Now HM Revenue and Customs.

Insolvent: a company is insolvent if it has insufficient funds (all of its assets) to pay its debts (all of its liabilities).

Intangible assets: assets of a non-physical or financial nature.

Inventory: goods manufactured or bought for resale by a business.

Invoice: a term describing an original document either issued by a business for the sale of goods on credit (a sales invoice) or received by the business for goods bought (a purchase invoice).

Journal(s): a book or set of books where your transactions are first entered.

Journal entries: a term used to describe the transactions recorded in a journal.

Ledger: a book in which entries posted from the journals are reorganised into accounts.

Leverage: see Gearing

Liabilities: this includes bank overdrafts, loans taken out for the business and money owed by the business to its suppliers. Liabilities are included on the right-hand side of the balance sheet and normally consist of accounts which have a credit balance.

Loss: see Net loss.

Management accounting: accounts and reports used by managers of a business (in any form they see fit – there are no rules) as opposed to financial accounts which are prepared for external users like tax authorities.

Mark-up: profit as a percentage of cost price.

Minority interest: ownership of a subsidiary company that is less than 50% and belongs to other investors.

Narrative: a comment appended to an entry in a journal. It can be used to describe the nature of the transaction, and often, in particular, where the other side of the entry went to (or came from).

Net loss: the value of expenses less sales assuming that the expenses are greater (i.e. if the profit and loss account shows a debit balance).

Net profit: the value of sales less expenses assuming that the sales are greater (i.e. if the profit and loss account shows a credit balance).

Net worth: see Equity.

Nominal accounts: a set of accounts held in the nominal ledger. They are termed 'nominal' because they don't usually relate to an individual person.

Nominal ledger: a ledger which holds all the nominal accounts of a business. Where the business uses a subsidiary ledger like the sales ledger to hold customer details, the nominal ledger will usually include a control account to show the total balance of the subsidiary ledger.

Non-current assets: these consist of anything which a business owns or buys for use within the business and which still retains a value at year end. They usually consist of major items like land, buildings, equipment and vehicles but can include smaller items like tools. See Depreciation.

Non-current liabilities: these usually refer to long-term loans (i.e. a loan which lasts for more than one year, such as a mortgage).

NPV: net present value.

Ordinary share: this is a type of share issued by a limited company. It carries the highest risk but usually attracts the highest rewards.

Original book of entry: see Books of prime entry.

Overheads: these are the costs involved in running a business, which are not traceable to any product or service. They consist entirely of expense accounts (e.g. rent, insurance, petrol, staff wages, etc.).

Paid-up share capital: the value of issued shares which have been paid for. See Called-up share capital.

P/E ratio: an equation which gives you a very rough estimate as to how much confidence there is in a company's shares (the higher it is the more confidence). The equation is: current share price multiplied by earnings and divided by the number of shares.

Personal accounts: these are the accounts of a business's customers and suppliers. They are usually held in the Sales and Purchase ledgers.

Petty cash: a small amount of money held in reserve (normally used to purchase items of small value where a cheque or other form of payment is not suitable).

Posting: the copying or transfer of entries from the journals to the ledgers.

Preference share: this is a type of share issued by a limited company. It carries a medium risk but has the advantage over ordinary shares in that preference shareholders get the first slice of the dividend 'pie' (usually at a fixed rate).

Prepayments: one or more accounts set up to account for money paid in advance (e.g. insurance, where part of the premium applies to the current financial year, and the remainder to the following year).

Prime book of entry: see Books of prime entry.

Profit margin: profit expressed as a percentage of selling price.

Provisions: one or more accounts set up to account for expected future payments (e.g. where a business is expecting a bill, but hasn't yet received it).

Purchase invoice: see Invoice.

Purchase ledger: a subsidiary ledger, which holds the accounts of a business's suppliers. A single control account is held in the nominal ledger which shows the total balance of all the accounts in the purchase ledger.

Raw materials: this refers to the materials bought by a manufacturing business in order to manufacture its products.

Receipt: a term typically used to describe confirmation of a payment – if you buy some petrol you will normally ask for a receipt to prove that the money was spent legitimately.

Reconciling: the procedure of checking entries made in a business's books with those on a statement sent by a third person (e.g. checking a bank statement against your own records).

Reducing-balance depreciation: an alternative to the commonly used straight-line (equal amounts per year) method. Rather than a fixed amount, a (fixed) percentage is charged every year. So, a £10,000 asset depreciation at 25% will be depreciated by £2,500 in the first year, but by £1,875 in the second year (i.e. 25% × £10,000 – £2,500). Compared to the straight-line method, depreciation is more heavily weighted towards early years.

Refund: if you return some goods you have just bought (for whatever reason), the company you bought them from may give you your money back. This is called a 'refund'.

Retained earnings: this is the amount of money held in a business after its owner(s) have taken their share of the profits.

Revenue: the sales and any other taxable income of a business (e.g. interest earned from money on deposit).

ROCE: Return on Capital Employed.

Sales: income received from selling goods or a service. See Revenue.

Sales ledger: a subsidiary ledger which holds the accounts of a business's customers. A control account is held in the nominal ledger (usually called a debtors' control account), which shows the total balance of all the accounts in the sales ledger.

Service: a term usually applied to a business which sells a service rather than manufactures or sells goods (e.g. an architect or a window cleaner).

Shareholders: the owners of a limited company or corporation.

Share premium: the extra paid above the face value of a share. Example: if a company issues its shares at £10 each, and later on you buy 1 share on the open market at £12, you will be paying a share premium of £2.

Shares: these are documents issued by a company to its owners (the shareholders) which state how many shares in the company each shareholder has bought and what percentage of the company the shareholder owns. Shares can also be called 'Stock'.

Shares issued: the number of shares a company has issued to shareholders.

Sole trader: the self-employed owner of a business.

Solvency: the ability of a business to pay its debts as they fall due.

Source document: an original invoice, bill or receipt to which journal entries refer.

Stakeholder: a party who affects, or can be affected by, a company's actions.

Stock: this can refer to the shares of a limited company (see Shares), or goods manufactured or bought for resale by a business.

Stockholders: see Shareholders .

Stock-taking: physically checking a business's stock for total quantities and value.

Stock valuation: valuing a stock of goods bought for manufacturing or resale.

Straight-line depreciation: depreciating something by the same (i.e. fixed) amount every year rather than as a percentage of its previous value. Example: a vehicle initially costs £10,000. If you depreciate it at a rate of £2,000 a year, it will depreciate to zero in exactly 5 years. See Depreciation.

T Account: a particular method of displaying an account where the debits and associated information are shown on the left, and credits and associated information on the right.

Tangible assets: assets of a physical nature. Examples include buildings, motor vehicles, plant and equipment, fixtures and fittings. See Intangible assets.

Transaction: two or more entries made in a journal which when looked at together reflect an original document such as a sales invoice or purchase receipt.

Trial balance: a statement showing all the accounts used in a business and their balances.

Turnover: the income of a business over a period of time (usually a year).

Value Added Tax: Value Added Tax, or VAT as it is usually called, is a sales tax which increases the price of goods. At the time of writing, the UK VAT standard rate is 15%, but this will revert to 17.5% from January 2010.

Wages: Payments made to the employees of a business for their work on behalf of the business. These are classed as expense items and must not be confused with 'drawings' taken by sole proprietors and partnerships (see Drawings).

Work in progress: the value of partly finished (i.e. partly manufactured) goods.

Write off: to depreciate an asset to zero in one go.

Glossary of accounting terms

Index

Main headings in **bold** are listed in the glossary.